Staying Stylish

Staying Stylish

CULTIVATING A CONFIDENT
LOOK, STYLE & ATTITUDE

CANDACE CAMERON BURE
NEW YORK TIMES BESTSELLING AUTHOR

WITH REBECCA MATHESON

ZONDERVAN®
.com

DEDICATION

To my grandmothers—

Grandma Jeanne:
You gave me an old, long velvet patchwork skirt when I was seven
years old that I wore for three days straight and didn't want to take off. It
was so ugly to everyone else, and yet I felt so cool and pretty in it.
I think it was the very piece that started my love for style and fashion.

Grandma Helen:
All those years playing beauty parlor in your living room with your
empty perfume bottles, soap tins, and brushes was my favorite time
spent with you. It made me love being a girl.

Contents

Clothes might just be what we wear,
but personal style helps us show who we are.

Introduction

I have loved fashion ever since I was a kid. It has always been so much more than clothing to me. It was a little part of life's big moments, like going back to school or finding the perfect outfit for an audition. It was a way to show my personality to the world. It was a way to feel beautiful and confident, to express myself, to stand apart from the crowd or to fit in seamlessly, to embrace every situation. In essence: it was an outward celebration of my inner self.

Even though my style has changed over the years, my belief that fashion is a way to express myself is one thing that has absolutely stayed the same. Clothes might just be what we wear, but personal style helps us show who we are.

FASHION HITS AND MISSES

My love of all things fashion began with colorful Converse sneakers and decorated denim. I loved to browse stores at the mall, searching for pieces

that had a standout element to them, like ruffled bloomers I could pair with a pleated black-and-white checkered skirt or colorful argyle tights worn with a simple black shorts suit. One of my college-aged babysitters once taught me how to DIY my own pair of distressed jeans, cutting them in a particular way so they'd fray just right at every hole and using bleach and the water hose in my backyard to create an acid-washed rinse. After that, I added rhinestones by hand for an extra-special touch. I actually wore those jeans on an episode of *Full House,* as my real-life clothes often influenced what I wore on the show. I loved to be a part of the costume process, and it was fun to add custom touches to my wardrobe. It taught me how appealing individual style can be. Including that one special standout factor in every outfit is something I still try to do today.

I've always found joy in trying new styles, but there were years when finding the right clothes became a lot harder.

Now, that's not to say that fashion has always come easily for me. I've always found joy in trying new styles, but there were years when finding the right clothes became a lot harder. My teenage years were especially difficult. I was growing up, my body was changing, and suddenly it wasn't as easy to find things that fit me well. I started to notice that what looked good on other people didn't always look good on me. Some clothes seemed to highlight my flaws more than my assets. Dresses that looked beautiful on the rack were unflattering once I put them on. Shirts didn't hang right, and pants that fit my waist didn't fit in the thighs. It was stressful and disheartening to try on beautiful pieces and everyday clothes that just did not work for my body type and me. I would flip through pages of couture fashion magazines and wonder, *How am I supposed to afford this? How can I wear this in my everyday life? Why can't I look like these models? I'll never be as tall or thin as they are.*

What I needed to cultivate wasn't a closet full of high-end runway looks but a wardrobe that was as dynamic and versatile as my life.

FINDING INSPIRATION

As I grew up, I realized my line of thinking was all wrong. Not only were the expectations being set by society damaging, but the clothes themselves were unrealistic. Many of those haute couture items were never meant to be worn in real life, and they certainly weren't representative of my actual life. I'm a laid-back California girl who spends most of my days working on set, going to meetings, hanging out at home with my husband and kids, or meeting friends for dinner. What I needed to cultivate wasn't a closet full of high-end runway looks but a wardrobe that was as dynamic and versatile as my life. My style isn't just about looking good or wearing designer brands; it's about looking like myself. I decided to throw out those magazines and started to look for inspiration in the world around me.

Inspiration wasn't hard to find. I started to notice outfits I saw women wearing on the street. I began to admire the way that women, both friends and strangers, wore clothes that seemed to highlight who they were and who they wanted to be. I really started paying attention to any detail that drew me in, whether it was the way buttons were arranged on a jacket or how a belt could pull together an entire outfit. I took note of textures I liked to wear and patterns that caught my eye as well as fabrics that were breathable over my skin. As I learned what I liked and what I didn't like, I slowly built a closet full of comfortable and flattering clothes that worked for me and my on-the-go lifestyle.

Fashion isn't about anyone else. It's about yourself—what you feel beautiful wearing and what makes you most comfortable, which leads to confidence.

BE TRUE TO YOU

As I became more comfortable in my own skin, I started to think differently about style. It's easy to look at the fashion world and feel rejected by it or to discount fashion and style as being superficial and shallow. But I decided to disregard those ways of thinking and the judgments and expectations attached to them. Fashion isn't about anyone else. It's about yourself—what you feel beautiful wearing and what makes you most comfortable, which leads to confidence.

THE ABSOLUTE BEST WAY

TO STAY STYLISH

IS TO STAY TRUE TO YOU.

Now with regard to my style, I focus on clothes that bring out the best parts of me. I look at getting dressed as putting on who I already am: a woman who loves her family, believes in God, works hard, enjoys being active, likes to travel, and finds joy and beauty in the moments in between.

So here's my first fashion tip in this book:

Fashion should be fun! It shouldn't be about how anyone else wants you to look, what you aren't, or where you fall short. In fact, it's exactly the opposite. Personal style is all about expressing who you are. It's about looking within yourself and finding the things you want to convey to the world. It's about embracing your inner beauty and showing that off. It's about being silly, being serious, being bold, being happy, being whole—being you. The absolute best way to stay stylish is to stay true to you. If you can follow that one simple rule, then you're already off to a good start!

MY STYLE JOURNEY

When I think about fashion these days, the first thing I think about is who I am inside. My sense of style is heavily influenced by my faith and my life. I am a wife to Val and mother to Natasha, Lev, and Maks, and I'm an actress, a producer, an author, and a businesswoman. I am someone who loves a low-key night in with friends and family but who always has to be prepared for a last-minute red-carpet event or to fly to a variety of cities to shoot a new movie in all types of weather. To design a closet that works for all the different roles I play, I had to pay attention to wardrobe basics. I had to learn how to balance an outfit. I had to master tricks that could make any piece in my closet look polished and tailored—even if that piece was just a comfy sweater.

Staying stylish is a journey, and one that I'm happily still on. I sincerely hope that sharing my style with you will help to inspire your own!

PART ONE

Fashion Is All About Balance

Balance is such an important ingredient for a full and happy life. Every morning when I wake up, I try to find balance in my day, so it's no surprise that balance plays such a key role in my wardrobe. I always strive to create a balanced look when I'm getting dressed. And one thing that really helps with that is having—you guessed it!— a balanced closet.

For me, a balanced closet means finding quality go-to pieces that form the foundation of my wardrobe, mixing in fun, trendy, and less expensive items, and keeping it all organized so it's easy to see everything I have and how it all fits together. This is not a precise art! My wardrobe is always a work in progress, but aiming for balance within it has made my life much easier. Now I know that I can always throw together an outfit at the last minute, find something to wear no matter what surprises my day has in store, and even go somewhere as casual as the grocery store while still looking cute and not sloppy. As anyone with kids and a busy schedule knows, that's not always easy!

My wardrobe is always a work in progress, but aiming for balance within it has made my life much easier.

I know you're probably thinking that balancing your closet sounds like a lot of work. It does take time, energy, and the ability to be brutally honest with yourself, but balancing your closet now will most definitely pay off later. At some point you've likely opened your closet and found it overflowing with a bunch of pieces that don't fit well, aren't quite your style, or just aren't your favorites, making it difficult to find the pieces you do love or quickly create an outfit that makes you feel phenomenal. The more organized and well thought out your wardrobe is, the less effort you will have to put into it on a daily basis. It will give you more time in the morning for important things, like prayer, exercise, or eating breakfast with your family, and it will streamline your style so it's easy to find an outfit no matter what kind of day you're facing. For the times when you do want to dress up a little more or be bolder with your style choices, it will make the experience fun and special.

Candace's Tips and Tricks:

Fill your closet with timeless basics that work well with each other. Make sure they are high quality and versatile enough to transition from casual to dressy and from day to night.

Fashion is a representation of who you are, so your closet should be a place where you go every morning to decide how you want to present yourself that day.

On the following pages, I've highlighted the basics that make up my closet. I wear them year after year, in constant rotation. In fact, I definitely wear one thing—if not several!—of these basics every day. These pieces are the foundation of my wardrobe, and though you may have a few different pieces that define your personal style or that work best with your figure, these are definitely options anyone could consider.

Tops

A lot of my basics fall into the category of tops, and that's because there are so many varieties and styles to choose from. There aren't many styles I avoid in this category—what can I say? I like having plenty of options! Since your top is the piece of clothing closest to your face, this is an especially important category. I avoid colors like chartreuse or bright orange since those colors can make my fair complexion look sallow. The same shades might look great in a print on a skirt or pair of trousers, but right next to my face, they just aren't as flattering. Instead I select a lot of white, black, and shades of blue, green, or pink because those colors complement my skin tone.

I like to have several color options available in the plain, everyday version of my favorites—tank tops, T-shirts, and button-downs—as well as a few special options of each. I suggest having more variety in this area of your wardrobe than in any other category. After all, you can wear the same pair of jeans with three different tops for three completely separate looks—a T-shirt for a casual look, a silk shell and blazer to look more professional, and a pretty blouse for date night. Once you decide on the styles and colors that make you feel your best, it's easy to stock up on great tops at any price point!

BUTTON-DOWN SHIRTS

I have to list button-down shirts as the first basic in my closet because they are a high-use staple for me! I love them so much because they are wildly versatile. You can wear button-downs alone or as a layering item. They can be tied at the waist, tucked into a skirt, or left untucked over pants. They can be professional or casual. From classic white to plaid flannel to oversized chambray, they are as customizable as they are diverse.

Candace's Tips and Tricks:

If you're going to wear a button-down shirt as a layering item, make your outfit look more polished by tucking in the first layer (usually a T-shirt or tank top under the button-down). This keeps the lines of the outfit clean. To make a casual look more modern and sophisticated, wear a more luxurious fabric like a heathered linen V-neck tee under an open rayon flannel. Pair with booties, and you're good to go!

If you're going to wear a button-down shirt as a layering item, make your outfit look more polished by tucking in the first layer.

T-SHIRTS

I live in my T-shirts! They are comfy, easy, and laid-back (all my favorite things!), yet somehow they always make their way into my dressed-up and tailored looks too. What can I say? I love T-shirts! Part of what makes them so indispensable to me is that they come in so many different categories: basic tees—hello there, black, white, and gray!—solids and patterns, crewneck and V-neck, graphic tees or cropped T-shirts for edgier looks, embellished tees in luxurious fabrics for dressier outfits, and then, of course, athletic T-shirts that wick away sweat. No matter the outfit, no matter the occasion, there is a T-shirt that is perfect for it!

Candace's Tips and Tricks:

To really dress up a T-shirt, wear it with statement jewelry. A long pendant or a wide-cuff bracelet can really elevate a cotton tee and take your whole look from plain Jane to stunning! Jewelry is also a great way to infuse your look with personality and make it unique to you—even if four other women in the room are also wearing black T-shirts and jeans. I usually select more minimalist pieces of jewelry like delicate chains and simple stud earrings, but I have a small collection of bigger, *wow* bangles and necklaces for just such an occasion.

My favorite

PLACES TO FIND BASIC T-SHIRTS:

NORDSTROM

TARGET

MACY'S

ZARA

GAP

MADEWELL

H&M

BLOOMINGDALES

My favorite

BRANDS ARE:

VINCE

PEACE LOVE WORLD

ALTERNATIVE APPAREL

SPLENDID

Z SUPPLY

TANK TOPS

The words *tank top* immediately bring to mind summer days and blue skies, but the reality is that tank tops are an ideal year-round layering item. Having the essential colors with a basic wide strap in your closet will help make your wardrobe more functional. I never hesitate to buy yet another tank in a great color when I find one because I know that I'll use it. Having vibrant and moody colors of tanks in various cuts, styles, and fabrics means I can pair a tank with anything for a new look!

A fitted tank in nude, black, or white is a great basic for layering under any top,

Candace's Tips and Tricks:

For a dressier look, try layering a lace or brushed silk racerback tank under a blazer, or for a more boho style, try tucking a slouchy jersey tank into a maxi skirt.

but it's the perfect match for a top with a neckline that reveals more than you're comfortable with. Plus, tanks are especially great to pack for trips since they are lightweight, don't take up a lot of space (more on that later!), and don't wrinkle easily.

BLOUSES

Blouses are some of the most standout pieces in the basics section of my closet. When you are going for a dressed-up or professional look, blouses pack a punch! They are inherently more polished and feminine than T-shirts or tank tops since they tend to be constructed from more luxurious fabrics like silk, satin, or linen with a focus on how they drape and accentuate your shape (or hide problem areas!).

My blouses tend to be more on trend, whether the craze of the season is a cold shoulder or a delicate ruffle. One of my favorite things about wearing a blouse is that I don't have to think through a lot of accessories or play up my hair and makeup as much since a great blouse is automatically the focal point of any outfit. Throw on a well-fitting blouse, and your work is pretty much done!

White blouses will always have a spot in my closet, but I also try to be intentional about picking blouses in fun colors. A mid-tone coral is almost universally flattering on all coloring. With my fairer skin, I love blues and greens too.

Candace's Tips and Tricks:

How do you know if a blouse fits well? The shoulder seam should hit the edge of your shoulder. More draping than that tells you it's too big, and most likely the underarm will be too roomy, leaving excess material that will add bulk and volume to your frame. On the other hand, make sure your blouse doesn't pull or gape across your bust when you move your arms. If it does, it's too small.

When you are going for a dressed-up

or professional look, blouses

pack a punch!

Bottoms & Dresses

My go-to categories for looking polished and professional are dresses, trousers, and skirts. I'm deeply in love with denim (more on that later!), but a perfectly tailored pair of trousers or a sleek pencil skirt definitely makes me feel powerful and confident walking into an important meeting or facing a press junket. And that matters! Choosing the right outfit is a little like putting on armor before going into battle. The right look can make you feel invincible, which is why it's so important to have a few power pieces in your wardrobe even if you are mostly a casual girl.

When it comes to feeling feminine, nothing beats a dress. There are so many amazing styles and options in this category, from red-carpet gowns to summer sundresses to structured sheaths. I know that a lot of women struggle to get the fit right with dresses. My advice is to find the cut that works best for you (an A-line works well for every body type!) and select that cut in a variety of fabrics and prints. For example, someone petite may get a satin sheath in a standout color for nights out, a white eyelet lace sheath for sunny days, and a tweed sheath for work. It's the same style, but the different fabrics, colors, and details keep these dresses from feeling too similar. You can always add less expensive dresses in other styles, but invest the bulk of your budget in your most flattering style.

PANTS

Nothing makes me feel like I'm ready to take on the world and get things done like a pair of black pants. Whether I'm heading into a power meeting, having an elegant dinner with friends, or feeling like I need a boost of confidence to get through my day, a nice pair of tailored pants always comes to the rescue. Once I slip them on with a sweater and a pair of heels, I immediately feel more in control and convinced I can accomplish anything. Fashion to the rescue!

Straight-leg suit pants fall in this category, but my favorites all have a special detail that is more interesting yet still classic, like a paper-bag waist, belt or sash, or tapered leg. My staples are a high-waisted pant paired with a cropped fitted sweater, which elongates my legs, and a mid- to low-rise ankle pant that can be worn casually with a T-shirt and flats or dressed up with a killer stiletto. Look for fabrics that won't wrinkle easily, like a wool blend or crepe. And don't be afraid to think beyond black. Colors like khaki, taupe, navy, and army green are just as versatile of neutrals.

Candace's Tips and Tricks:

Tailoring is important when it comes to pants. Focus on the fit rather than the actual size. Sizes vary greatly among different brands, so try not to get too hung up on the number itself. You may have to try on a lot of different pairs before you find the cut that works best for your body, but it's worth all those dressing-room hours when you have a pair that makes you feel like a million bucks!

SKIRTS

Skirts are an instant way to look classy, feminine, and pretty! Since they come in a variety of styles and shapes, it's easy to wear them no matter where you're going. My personal must-haves are A-line skirts in mini and midi lengths and pencil skirts. These are universally flattering skirts, no matter how big or small your curves, that create nice lines and can be worn in both casual and formal settings. You can easily dress down a full or pleated midi skirt with a tank top or T-shirt and sandals or dress it up with a heel or pointed-toe flat and a crisp button-down. Wear a solid-colored pencil skirt with a nice blouse for professional settings or a high-waisted one with a silk camisole and cardigan for a cocktail event. Skirts are the perfect item to play with for adding prints like florals, geometrics, or stripes as well as textures like tweed, jacquard, linen, or knit to your outfit.

With skirts, balance really matters. If a skirt is more fitted to your body, then wear a looser top to create a chic silhouette. If a skirt is more full and flowing, then the top should be fitted. And last but not least, don't forget about your waist! Most skirts look best when paired with a top that's tucked in or cropped at the top of the skirt's waistline. Adding a belt can draw attention to your waist, creating your best shape. Balance. It's everything.

With skirts, balance really matters.

Candace's Tips and Tricks:

Skirts can be worn in the winter too! Seasonless skirts can be paired
with a sweater and layered with tights. Look for cotton blends that keep
you comfortable as you transition from season to season.

DRESSES

I turn to dresses whenever I want to feel extra feminine or I want an effortless and easy outfit. It doesn't get much more un-fussy than a single piece! And dresses are universally flattering. No matter how tall or short you are or where your curves fall, there's a style of dress that will work for you and make you feel gorgeous. My three go-tos are:

Candace's Tips and Tricks:

If you have thicker arms and want to wear sleeveless dresses, a little alteration can make them more flattering. Starting from the outside of the shoulders, take in the fabric an inch or two to make the straps thinner.

(1) *THE SUNDRESS:* I have dozens of sundresses in my closet in all different cuts, colors, and styles. Maybe it's because I'm a California girl, but I can't pass a rack of sundresses in a store without checking them out! There's something about them that takes me back to being a little girl spending her days on the beach, but they also make me feel like my most beautiful self. I'm always on the look-out for details like a flutter sleeve or hidden pockets. Can I get an amen?!

A jersey maxi dress will keep you cool, comfortable, and looking good even in the worst of the summer heat. I'm also particular to halter-cut dresses that show off my strong shoulders. But if I had to pick only one sundress to wear for the rest of my life, it would be a vintage classic style with a modern twist in a bright sunshine yellow like you might find at Anthropologie.

It doesn't get much more unfussy

than a single piece!

(2) *THE WHITE DRESS:* I think there's something really elegant and beautiful about a simple white dress. I'm not knocking a little black dress, but a bright-white dress always stands out! I focus on the cut and shape of the dress to add that special element to an otherwise understated look. For example, I'd pick a white peplum dress that falls below the knee for evening wear or a white eyelet shift dress for church and Sunday brunch.

③ *THE A-LINE DRESS:* No closet is complete without an A-line dress! This is a style of dress that any woman can wear. The fit-and-flare cut can give the illusion of a smaller waist and camouflage wider hips, and it can also create a waistline for those with a more rectangular shape. Whether an A-line dress is patterned or black, cotton or linen, it's a universally flattering basic that can be worn anywhere.

Denim, Denim, Denim

That's right—this section is a big one for me! I love denim from the bottom of my heart. Growing up in Southern California, it was pretty much a given that denim was the fabric of my childhood. Both on- and offscreen, I've worn every version of denim imaginable, from overalls and colored denim pants to rompers, jean jackets, and jean skirts. I can measure years by what denim piece I was wearing at any given time. Let's just say that not much has changed! My denim choices may be more sophisticated now, but it's still the one fabric that makes me feel most comfortable and most like myself.

My denim choices may be more sophisticated now, but it's still the one fabric that makes me feel most comfortable and most like myself.

So how do you make denim sophisticated? How do you wear it in every possible situation without looking too casual? How do you incorporate it into even the most professional and polished of outfits? The answers to these questions all lie with the brightest star in the denim universe: the perfect pair of jeans.

Jeans

There might not be any item in a wardrobe more personal than a pair of jeans. Jeans conjure up a million images for me: summer nights, barbecues and picnics, trips up the coast, California sunsets, evenings spent around the table with my husband and kids. Whether they are distressed and faded or high waisted in a dark wash, there's no denying that jeans are quintessentially all-American. They also happen to be really comfortable!

There might not be any item in a wardrobe more personal than a pair of jeans.

HIGH-WAISTED JEANS

It's funny that a cut of jeans that was so popular when I was a kid has come back in style. Fashion, full circle! I can guess what you may be thinking: *Mom jeans?!* But hear me out. High-waisted jeans can be flattering on everyone. They highlight the waist if you're an hourglass shape and tuck in a tummy if you're not. If you're petite like I am, the high waist creates a straight line through the leg, elongating your frame.

My favorite way to wear them is with a bodysuit or tucked-in shirt as the base layer, a button-down shirt as the top layer, and a pair of booties.

Candace's Tips and Tricks:

If you want to try a high waist but are afraid of looking too dated, stick to jeans with a 9-inch rise. This mid-level rise isn't as dramatic.

SKINNY JEANS IN A DARK WASH

In my opinion, this is the must-have pair of jeans for every woman! This is how to look really polished in denim. There is nothing that can't be worn with a pair of dark-wash skinny jeans. They look good on everyone, and they are my first choice when I need a dressier look.

I love to pair skinny jeans with a blazer, T-shirt, and heels. Skinny jeans are also ideal to tuck into boots with a shaft that hits at mid-calf or higher since they aren't bulky.

Candace's Tips and Tricks:

If you find skinny jeans to be uncomfortable, you may want to try some with more stretch in them, typically 98 percent cotton and 2 percent Lycra. Straight-leg jeans can work if you feel that skinny jeans aren't for you. Straight legs are fitted at the waist, hips, and thighs, but they remain the same width down to the ankles instead of tapering in like skinnies. As long as you choose a slimmer straight leg, it has a similar effect. They also do a nice job of creating the illusion of a longer leg since the bottom hem is slightly wider than the hem on a skinny jean.

Go-To Brands

A FEW OF MY
favorite
BRANDS OF JEANS:

MOTHER

FRAME

HUDSON

PAIGE

J BRAND

AG

GOOD AMERICAN

LEVI'S

MADEWELL

TOPSHOP

I know most of these brands tend to be on the more expensive side, but the quality and fit can't be beat. These jeans have lasted me for years and years, and with how frequently I wear them, it's worth it to me to invest in pairs I truly love. It's also important to me that most of the brands I mentioned are mad e in the USA and manufactured in Southern California.

Finding jeans is no easy task. I can't tell you how many jeans I have to try on every time I want a new pair. That's why when you find a brand and cut that works for you, you may want to buy several in different washes!

DISTRESSED JEANS

I can't help it! I love the faded and damaged look of distressed jeans. Maybe there's still a little bit of that girl in me who ripped, cut, and bleached her own pair as a kid. Or maybe it's just that distressed jeans are perfect for California, with their laid-back vibe that has the slightest bit of edge.

Either way, I find myself wearing distressed jeans no matter the season. When it's warm out, I wear them with strappy brown sandals and a classic white T-shirt for a clean, crisp look. On cold days, I wear them over tights and pair them with booties and a suede jacket.

CROPPED JEANS

No jeans look as good with a simple pair of white sneakers or slides as cropped jeans. I like the athletic feel of this combination. If the hem is fitted to the leg and falls only a few inches above the ankle, you can also pair cropped jeans with Chelsea boots in the winter. Culottes or wide-leg crops work well with wedges or block-heel sandals.

Candace's Tips and Tricks:

To avoid looking like you're revisiting your teenage years, forgo distressed jeans with too many holes in them. Instead, opt for details like frayed thread and a light-wash treatment.

FASHION HACK

How to Bring New Life to Old Jeans

Do you have a pair of jeans in your closet that you love, but the cut has gone out of style? Or maybe they've just started to look a little old and worn-out?

It takes time to find a pair of jeans that fit me well in my butt, waist, and thighs, so I try to keep every pair in rotation for as long as possible. That's why I learned how to bring new life to an old pair of jeans. To do this simple trick, all you need is a pair of fabric scissors and a little creativity.

Take the scissors and cut the hem of the jeans high in the front about 1 to 2 inches above your ankle, but keep the back hem an inch or two below that cut. The frayed hem and asymmetrical cut that will immediately bring a fresh, edgy new look to your jeans.

Want a pair of cropped jeans without spending a dime? Simply cut a regular-length pair of jeans a few inches above the hem, roll twice, and you've got yourself a new pair of cropped, cuffed jeans.

DENIM SHORTS

If I could, I would spend all summer wearing denim shorts. That being said, lots of my friends have commented on how tricky it is to find a flattering pair of denim shorts. I have to agree—it may even be harder than finding the right pair of jeans, which is saying a lot!

I think the problem is that if denim shorts are too short, they age women. But if denim shorts are too long, they also age women. So the key is to find a pair of shorts that hit at the waist and end slightly above the mid-thigh.

I love shorts with a rolled-up cuff at the bottom like these Madewell ones I'm wearing, but nothing says Malibu like a frayed pair of cutoff Levi's. Add black sneakers and a white top for immediate comfort and happiness!

Candace's Tips and Tricks:

I've found that trying on denim shorts that are 1 to 2 sizes bigger than my normal size, especially in a boyfriend fit, helps me find the right length. The shorts I'm pictured in are 2 inches larger than my typical waist size, but because they are high waisted, they don't fall off my hips. The bigger size gives these "short" shorts more length, ultimately giving me a perfect fit.

DENIM JUMPSUIT

All right, hear me out. A denim jumpsuit or romper can be a great basic. That's why I've worn different versions of them on every season of *Fuller House,* and they're always the piece of clothing fans ask about. A jumpsuit is an easy outfit by itself—just throw on a simple pair of sandals—and so well structured that it looks instantly streamlined. The trick is to avoid cuts that show too much skin or scream "juniors' section." Don't get me wrong—the juniors' section is full of cool, fun pieces, but a romper is youthful enough without adding extra teen-oriented embellishments or cutouts.

With jumpsuits, getting the right fit and the right amount of coverage is key! That means trying on lots of jumpsuits—so don't get discouraged if the first few you try on aren't quite right for you. If you keep trying, you are sure to find one that makes you feel fun and on trend.

DENIM JACKET

The first denim jacket I ever wore as a kid was on *Full House.* I immediately fell in love with the shiny copper buttons, light wash, and slightly oversized fit. It made me feel comfortable but cool. Tough but pretty. Strong and excited. Any clothing item that can do all that is definitely a keeper!

I wear a denim jacket year-round. It's one of those clothing items that only gets better with age. A little fraying and a mark here or there somehow only give it more character. And bonus—the longer you wear a denim jacket, the more comfortable it becomes. I wear my denim jackets over everything; the right one can even be worn with a cocktail dress!

With jumpsuits, getting the right fit and the right amount of coverage is key!

Classic Outerwear

Denim jackets are the perfect transition to my next category of basics: outerwear. I can't emphasize this enough: outerwear doesn't just top off an outfit—the right jacket or coat can also add an element of polish and really complete a look. Whether you live in a frosty climate that demands wool coats or a more temperate climate that calls for wrap sweaters, outerwear is the ingredient that finishes off and perfects your day-to-day style. Plus, what woman doesn't love a clothing item that can be thrown over everything else to instantly make her look chic and ready for the day?

Outerwear is also one of those areas where spending a little more money on quality pieces goes a long way. Since coats and jackets are such defining elements of an outfit, and because they are worn so much in a season, it's important to have pieces that can really hold up to wear and tear while keeping you warm.

Outerwear is also one of those areas where spending a little more money on quality pieces goes a long way.

WRAP SWEATER

There might not be anything as comforting in any closet as a sweater. I just love how cozy they make me feel, like I'm instantly at home. Wrap sweaters are especially perfect for California weather, where even sunny days can sometimes be surprisingly chilly. I also love wrap sweaters for when I travel, since I'm often traveling between different climates—and airplanes can be cold!

For a fall look, pair a patterned wrap sweater with a long-sleeved black turtleneck, distressed jeans, and tan booties with a slight heel.

BLAZER

Blazers are all about shape. The way they nip in at the waist and are a little wider at the shoulders make them a power piece in any woman's wardrobe. The structure of a good blazer gives the illusion of an hourglass figure if you don't have curves or can disguise a bit of a tummy for a slimming effect. They can really elevate an otherwise laid-back outfit. I tend to stick to solid neutral colors like black, navy, olive green, beige, and cream so they work with patterned blouses, printed trousers, and a rainbow of colors. Blazers are the perfect topper for any outfit, including jeans, dresses, skirts, and, of course, the power suit.

Candace's Tips and Tricks:

With most outfits, sticking to the same color palette really helps up the sophistication factor. Try separates that are the same color but have a variety of textures, or try subtle variations of the same shade.

How to Dress Up a Casual Outfit

When it comes to formal or casual wear, I will pick casual any day of the week! I really believe in being comfortable and wearing clothes that feel as good as they look. But some days require both types of outfits, like when I have to help my kids with a school project, then run to a meeting. In this case, I like to keep my base outfit simple and add accessories that can make it either more casual or dressier.

A navy-and-white striped T-shirt with jeans is a great base outfit. If I wear it with pink slip-ons, it makes for a fun and bright day look that is easy to move around in. If I need to dress it up, I just swap slip-ons for embellished heels and add a classic black blazer. No costume change needed!

UTILITY JACKET

A great utility jacket, sometimes called a military jacket, is as versatile as a jean jacket but won't give you denim overload if you're already wearing it elsewhere. I have a green utility jacket in my closet that I wear all the time. I love how functional it is with plenty of pockets and zippers, while also looking sharp with clean lines. The added studs on the pockets give it a tough vibe, but the cotton fabric screams effortless. I wear it so much that I keep it hanging by the door, just in case I need to grab it on my way out.

Candace's Tips and Tricks:

You can wear utility jackets in professional settings too! Look for a lightweight jacket with more tailored details, like a drape front or a hidden drawstring to cinch in the waist.

Where to Spend and Where to Save

When it comes to shopping, I find the cost-per-wear rule to be helpful. Sometimes items that seem really expensive turn out to be less expensive than cheaper clothing or accessory options when you think about how much use you will get out of them and how long they will last. Wearing one pricier, flattering, high-quality jacket for five years might cost the same as or less than buying five cheaper jackets that you will wear for only one year each.

Plus, saving up for a piece of clothing will help ensure that you aren't making an impulse purchase. If you have to save for an item or buying it takes up your entire clothing budget for a time period, it forces you to make sure that you really love it and will wear it over and over again.

SPEND: I invest in classic pieces that will stay in style even as time passes. Spending more money on high-quality clothing pays off, since I get so much wear out of these items. I look for items with natural fibers like cashmere, wool, 100 percent cotton, and silk, which stand the test of time, and avoid synthetic fibers like polyester and modal (a type of rayon), which wear out as quickly as the season. Having a few expensive pieces that really dress up an outfit also makes getting dressed easier. For me, my "spend" items are outerwear, jeans, and handbags.

SAVE: Seasonal and trendy pieces are good items to save money on, since they are shuffled through in a season and they tend to go out of fashion much more quickly than classic pieces. My "save" items are summer dresses, rompers, trendy tops, and skirts and pants that are the cut or embellishment of the moment.

Sometimes items that seem really expensive turn out to be less expensive than cheaper clothing or accessory options when you think about how much use you will get out of them and how long they will last.

Winter Outerwear

Even though I live in California, I often find myself in colder locales when I'm filming. Between New York in the winter and snowy sets in Vancouver, I've had to master the art of layering. It helps to have a base outfit that can be paired with several different coats and jackets.

My go-to base outfit for winter is a patterned sweater (I love stripes!), black skinny jeans, and over-the-knee black boots.

LEATHER JACKET

On more temperate days, I wear my winter look with a leather jacket. I really like the classic moto jacket since the hardware and open collar make a statement and give any look some edge.

I love the soft, buttery feel of a vintage leather jacket, but I also love all the great faux options, which are wallet- and conscience-friendly.

Candace's Tips and Tricks:

If the classic moto jacket is too tough-looking for you, you may still be able to find a style that works for you. Look for a lightweight jacket in a light color, like tan or blush pink, that's collarless and more fitted to the body. Some of the vegan moto jacket options also mix materials, such as knit for the sleeves, which can soften the look.

WOOL COAT

Then, of course, there are those mornings when it's too cold for anything except a heavy coat! In that case, I really love one that makes a statement, like this long purple wool coat that ties in the front. My investment would be a below-the-knee coat so it covers a dress but allows for ease when walking and shows off my shoes. It's more difficult to find a great coat in this length, so it's a good place to spend a little bit more. There are often a lot of cute shorter coats on the racks, so you can probably save a little there! It's all in the details. Find that standout element like a shawl collar, tie-waist, belt, or faux-fur detail.

Candace's Tips and Tricks:

Consider the length when buying your next coat. A three-quarter-length coat will keep you warm and cover your derriere, but it tends to be a more casual length, worn best with pants.

Shoes

Shoes are the easiest way to dress an outfit up or down. They can make an outfit look cute and athletic (sneakers!), laid-back and casual (sandals!), or chic and powerful (heels!). There have been plenty of mornings when I've built my outfit around which kind of shoes I want to wear that day. As I've gotten older, I've finally learned how to hit the balance between comfort and style when it comes to shoes. These are my picks that make the cut.

I've finally learned how to hit the balance between comfort and style when it comes to shoes.

SNEAKERS

I live in sneakers! I loved them as a teenager, and I love them now as a working mom. Not only are sneakers comfortable and good for the health of your feet, but they can also be cute, fun, and trendy. To find sneakers that appear more fashionable than athletic, focus on slim and sleek looks in solid colors (neutral or brights!) or that have a fun factor like glitter or metallic details. Some of my favorite fashionable brands are Converse, Golden Goose, Common Projects, and Steve Madden. My favorite athletic brands for working out are Brooks, Nike, Adidas, and Asics.

WEDGES

Wedges, in my opinion, are the ideal balance of comfort and added height and a great alternative for women who don't feel comfortable in pumps or stilettos. A lot of wedges even have extra padding on the insoles, which is a nice bonus! Everyone can wear them and walk in them, and they're perfect for elevating even the most casual outfits without looking overdone. Wedge heels are made in every style shoe, from winter boots to summer sandals. Espadrilles and strappy suede and leather wedges take over my closet in the summertime, and I wear them with everything from jean shorts to elegant maxi dresses. Oh, and D. J. Tanner is particularly partial to wedges (wink).

Candace's Tips and Tricks:

Separate your fashionable sneakers from your athletic ones.
Running shoes and cross-trainers should be worn while working out,
not hanging out. Pairs that are bulky or have too many neon colors
will look like they belong in the gym. My favorite athletic brands for
working out are Brooks, Nike, Adidas, and Asics.

HEELS

Sometimes you just really need the sophistication that heels bring to an outfit. They add glamour to otherwise casual wardrobe staples like jeans and T-shirts and are must-haves for formal wear. Because I'm such a shoe girl—they really are the item I love in fashion above all else—I have no restrictions on what I look for when it comes to stilettos. Tie-up, strappy, colorful patterns, jewel embellishments, metallic, quirky heel shapes, block heels, open-toe, closed-toe, pointed-toe, and rounded-toe, I love them all!

Candace's Tips and Tricks:

The heels in my closet that work with almost every outfit and that I travel with most are simple open-toe strappy heels (Stuart Weitzman's the Nudist sandal in a 4.5-inch heel) in nude and black and pointed closed-toe pumps (Stuart Weitzman's Curvia pump in a 4-inch heel) in nude and black. If you get those four basics, they should easily pair with everything in your wardrobe, no matter what the current trend may be.

SHOES ARE THE EASIEST WAY

TO DRESS AN OUTFIT UP OR DOWN.

Red-Carpet Guide

I know dressing up for a red carpet might sound like a dream come true. Though there are parts of it that I love and embrace; there are also parts of it that can be incredibly nerve-racking! There are cameras and flashbulbs everywhere, and everyone is reporting on what and whose designs you're wearing and what it says about who you are as a person. It can be easy to go wrong, even when you think you've done everything right.

But whether you're walking the red carpet, dressing up for a fancy date night, or attending a formal event, the most important thing is that you're wearing what makes you feel beautiful.

My Favorite Red-Carpet Looks Through the Years

It took years for me to figure out what kind of dress would make me feel most like myself on a red carpet. It wasn't just about feeling pretty; it was about feeling comfortable, balanced, and confident. I had to learn how to pick out a dress that would work for an event. That doesn't mean I don't take fashion risks or try something out of my comfort zone, but after (so many!) trial-and-error fashion moments, these are the elements I tend to look for now.

JEWEL TONES. I love dresses in jewel-tone colors like bright fuchsia, sapphire, and emerald green. Since I lean toward dresses with simple and classic cuts, picking a bright color is a way for me to add that standout element to my outfit. Plus, it gives me a way to have fun with high-fashion looks.

DRESS COLORS THAT MATCH THE SEASON. I know this rule might seem a little old-fashioned, but I like to celebrate each time of year by sticking to palettes that coordinate with the respective

season. At a red-carpet event, there's nothing worse than feeling like you stand out in a negative way. So in spring and summer I stick to lighter colors, and I choose darker colors for autumn and winter.

DRESSES THAT LEAVE A LITTLE TO THE IMAGINATION. I avoid dresses that are too revealing (for me). The "for me" part of that sentence is so important. The idea of modesty varies from person to person, and it's all about what each person feels comfortable wearing. In my case, I try to find dresses that highlight only one part of my body at a time, like my shoulders or my legs. Then I have mostly everything else covered. It makes me feel elegant, but not exposed or uncomfortable. It's important for me to move around a little when trying on a dress. A dress might look great while I'm standing still, but what about when I lean forward to get out of the car? Or sit down? Or dance? No one wants a wardrobe malfunction while trying to have a good time!

This green Michael Costello gown hits all my marks for the perfect red-carpet dress!

Hidden Figures

What's underneath the prettiest of dresses isn't always as gorgeous as what's on the outside. Undergarments can make or break any outfit, so it's important to find the right ones to help flatter your shape and the garments you're wearing.

① Shapewear is particularly helpful to slim and smooth your body and helps keep it tucked in in all the right places.

② There are endless bra options like strapless, backless, seamless, adhesive cups, corset, and deep-V plunge to keep "the girls" looking good and in place in any style dress or top.

③ Using tools and tricks like double-sided fashion tape can help fabric stay in place so you aren't accidentally exposed.

④ Placing cutlets in your bra may give you an added boost if placed underneath and toward the outside of your breasts or help separate them if placed underneath, toward the inside.

⑤ The most gorgeous special-occasion dress can be ruined by a bad undergarment choice (visible panty lines—gasp!), so it's important to try on your ensemble ahead of time with your planned undergarments and study yourself critically from every angle to ensure there are no lines or bulges you can eliminate with different underthings.

⑥ Having a friend take a few pictures of hard-to-see spots is a good option if you struggle to see everything in the mirror! This will help ensure you feel confident for your big event.

A Peek Inside My Closet

Now that I've shared my wardrobe staples, from winter days to red-carpet nights, I want to introduce you to the place where these clothes live: my closet! I've spent a lot of time making my closet a space that is functional, easy, and most of all, inspiring. The first step to reaching these goals is to focus on organization.

Candace's Tips and Tricks:

I organize my closet by category: tops, jeans, long dresses and pieces, skirts, shorts, and outerwear. Within each category, I color coordinate, starting with dark colors on the left and gradually working toward lighter shades of color on the right. This makes it easy to find specific pieces of clothing, and it gives me a simple overall view of what I have.

SEASONAL STORAGE

I like to pack away clothes that are out of season, storing them in canvas bags with a clear top or sides for easy viewing. Living in Los Angeles, I often don't need my winter clothes unless I'm traveling. Packing away sweaters and other items gives me more space in my closet so I can clearly see my warm-weather options.

In the past when I've lived in cities with four seasons, I did a complete closet changeover twice per year, in spring and fall. I always thought it was really fun to open the storage bags every year and rediscover pieces I hadn't worn in a while. When items are out of sight for an extended period of time, they can seem brand-new when you see them again. Plus, taking the time to unpack and rehang each item helps me spot basics that need to be repaired or replaced, refamiliarize myself with my options for that season, and spot gaps in my wardrobe that can be filled with a few new trendy items. It's an easy (and cheap!) way for your wardrobe to feel fresh and revitalized!

Candace's Tips and Tricks:

I'm a big follower of the one-year rule. If I haven't worn something in a year, whether that's because it doesn't fit, it's off trend, or I'm just not able to pair it with other pieces in my closet, then I pass it along to a friend or donate the item to charity.

SENTIMENTAL ITEMS

The one category of items in my closet that I really tend to hold on to are sentimental pieces. Whether they are pieces that were given to me

by someone important in my life or pieces that I associate with a special memory, I consider personal items like these to be keepers. I purchased several of the costumes I wore on *Dancing with the Stars* because of their sentimental value. I realize I may not ever wear my custom-made Ariel outfit unless I'm dressing up for Halloween or a children's *Little Mermaid*–themed party, but it makes my heart swell just knowing I have it. And just like my wedding dress is boxed, preserved, and stored for safe keeping, so are some of my oldest pairs of jeans that were well worn and loved. I know it might go against the rules of organization to hold on to things that aren't actively being used, but in this case, I make an exception.

My closet is a representation of me, after all!

A FEW OF MY FAVORITE THINGS

An outfit starts with classic wardrobe staples, but it takes on a whole new life with accessories! They are an easy way to add personality to any outfit. Unlike many clothing items, accessories can last for years, so it's worth taking the time to really find pieces that feel representative of your identity and your personality. I've been fortunate enough to design my own jewelry with some of the brands below. These companies are standouts because not only do they design beautiful and unique pieces, but they give back tremendously to either those who make them or to nonprofit organizations.

(1) *31 BITS:* The "31" comes from Proverbs 31 in the Bible, which describes a hard-working wife and mother who cares for the needs of her loved ones. The company makes beads from "bits" of paper! Their mission is to use hand-crafted jewelry to help people earn a decent wage. The work opportunities 31 Bits offers these artisans gives customers a chance to buy products that were fairly made. Artisans get more than just income. They have access to counseling, health care, and education that is funded by their sales. That means that every purchase you make directly affects these amazing employees and their families. I love their jewelry almost as much as I love their mission!

I created these pieces with 31 Bits along with my daughter, Natasha. You've seen me wear many of their pieces on Season 3 of *Fuller House*.

(2) *BENEVOLENCE LA:* Every product sold benefits a charity. Benevolence LA is based on the idea that small acts of generosity can lead to dramatic results. And it's happening!

I created a line of rose quartz pieces that benefit Lollipop Theater Network, which brings the magic of movies nationwide to children to hospitals.

POLISHING OFF AN OUTFIT

Working in Hollywood and seeing the behind-the-scenes tricks of different costume departments on sets, I know what a production getting dressed can be! Sometimes you have the right basics, the right accessories, and the right shoes, but for some reason the outfit looks a little off. What are the magic ingredients that make an outfit really sing?

A STEAMER. It can be a high-powered standing steamer that stays in your closet or a portable handheld one you can travel with or put in your desk at work. They all achieve the same thing: making sure there are no wrinkles in an outfit and that your fabric looks as fresh in the evening as it did in the morning. Steaming really does make a huge difference, and it often takes less time than ironing.

ALTERATIONS. Clothes rarely fit perfectly off the rack. No two bodies are the same, and clothes are usually mass-produced in standard sizes that won't work for everyone. It's ridiculous to think that our arms are all the same length or that our waists measure the same number of inches around. After all, God made each of us exactly as we are, and those differences are

Candace's Tips and Tricks:

For more complicated alterations, and for those investment pieces that are classic and high quality, a tailor is worth the investment. It's better to have one piece of clothing that fits you perfectly and will last for years than to have a bunch of clothes that are less expensive and don't fit well at all.

worth celebrating! If we were all a perfect size 4, the world would be a pretty boring place. So buying a piece of clothing is really only a starting point.

In my case, I am considered petite, coming in at a towering 5 foot 2. Almost every piece of clothing I buy is too long, especially the sleeves and pant legs. I originally learned how to hand-sew to reattach buttons that would come off, but being able to adjust the length of my pants and shirts comes in handy. It may seem like these things are too complicated to be done at home and too expensive to have done every time you buy a new piece of clothing, but that's not true. Clothing is so customizable. Mastering a few easy tricks—like using safety pins to hem sleeves in a pinch, or using double-sided fashion tape for everything from hemming pants to making sure there are no gaps between the buttons in a button-down shirt—are easy at-home fixes that anyone can master and won't hurt your budget either.

Polish is all in the details!

Candace's Tips and Tricks:

Another one of my favorite at-home tricks is to use double-sided tape behind the tail end of a belt. The tape forces the belt to lie flat so that the belt is in one clean line, which makes the outfit look sharp.

SOME DAYS THE BEST LOOK

IS THE SIMPLEST LOOK.

SIMPLICITY AS A GUIDING RULE

As much as I love outfits with fun details that help me stand out in a crowd, I also really believe in the beauty of simplicity. Sometimes there's nothing that makes me feel as pretty as a T-shirt. Maybe it's because when an outfit is stripped down to just the simplest details, the focus is on the person wearing it. I've seen so many women in my own life follow simplicity as a guiding rule, and I've come to believe that some days the best look is the simplest look. I'm talking about those mornings when you just get out of bed, apply tinted moisturizer, pull your hair into a ponytail, and put on a simple shift dress or a pair of jeans and a sweatshirt—simple pieces in basic colors that are not dressed up or decorative but somehow define perfectly who you are in that moment. Just yourself. Plain . . . and simple.

Fashion on the Go

Travel has always been a very big part of my life. When I was a kid, I was lucky to travel all around the world, so I learned early on that it's one of the most important experiences anyone can have. Travel introduces people to a wide range of different cultures and lifestyles. It shapes and challenges us. It offers us a new perspective on the world. Traveling really is one of the most rewarding things anyone can do, but it also takes a little practice to be an efficient and well-organized traveler—especially when it comes to clothes!

It takes a little practice to be an efficient and well-organized traveler—especially when it comes to clothes!

More than once, I have been the traveler with far too many suitcases stuffed with clothes I don't end up wearing and things I don't end up using. It took visiting many different countries and living abroad with my husband, Val, to get me to the point I've reached today. Now I know what to pack, how to pack it, and how to keep it all in order. No small accomplishment!

Here's how I handle fashion in transit.

PACKING MY SUITCASE

I am one of those people who loves to pack! Maybe it's because I look at my suitcase as a small and portable version of my closet that I'm curating and organizing for a specific locale. It's exciting to look at my wardrobe and see what possibilities it holds for a new destination. Traveling has this way of making old clothes feel like new by giving them a fresh context and different possibilities. With a little focus and a lot of organization, packing really can be an exciting step in the traveling process.

Candace's Tips and Tricks:

A good suitcase doesn't have to be expensive! I prefer a hard-sided suitcase because it's the most durable, and four wheels with 360-degree spinning are a must.

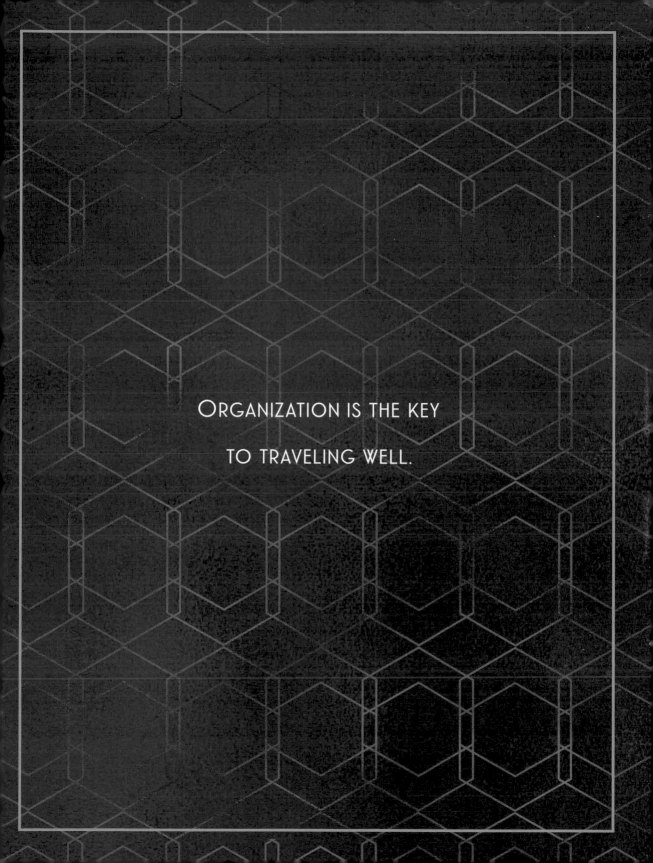

ORGANIZATION IS THE KEY

TO TRAVELING WELL.

Organization is the key to traveling well. Because so much of my travel revolves around work commitments, I know that how well a suitcase is organized can make or break a trip. I have to be able to step off a plane, head to a hotel, open my suitcase, and quickly pick out an outfit that will be as wrinkle-free as possible and ready to wear.

ORGANIZING MY SUITCASE

I TRY ON MY CLOTHES! There's nothing worse than having arrived at your destination and opening up your suitcase prepared to wear something, and it doesn't fit. Maybe the item shrank a bit in the wash; maybe there's a snag you didn't see. Maybe you're just feeling bloated and know it isn't going to be comfortable to wear that day or the material isn't as soft as you remembered. So I try on all my outfits before they get packed in my suitcase to ensure everything is what I'll actually want to wear.

I STICK TO ONE COLOR PALETTE. No matter the trip, no matter the time of year, when I pack I always choose one color palette for all my clothes. This requires me to bring less clothing overall because I can pair all the pieces together in different combinations—a minimum number of clothing items for a maximum number of outfits! For example, my winter go-to color palette is black, white, and beige. Since they are all neutrals that work together, the pairing options are endless. And all these pieces will match with the same hat, printed scarf, and shoes. In the spring and summer, I tend to stick to whites, denim, and one color pop, like variations of pink: soft pink, bubble gum, and fuchsia. That means I won't pack anything with red because most likely I'd have to throw in an additional pair of shoes and accessories to coordinate it all.

I ROLL CLOTHING. It's true what everyone says. Rolling clothing doesn't just save space; it also ensures fewer wrinkles.

I ORGANIZE MY SUITCASE BY ITEM, JUST LIKE MY CLOSET. I know that many people like to organize their suitcase by outfit (with the first outfit they need packed on top and outfits for the following days beneath in consecutive order). However, when I try to pack like that, I quickly find that the system doesn't work for me past day one. My schedule is too unpredictable! Travel can be full of surprises, and itineraries can change. So it's easier for me to organize my suitcase by packing the same types of items together: shirts, pants, dresses, jeans, and so forth. I only have to take one glance to know what pieces I have with me and how I can pair them.

My Airport Outfit

P art of packing well is mastering the airport outfit. It has always been important to me to look nice at the airport. I've never been one of those people who opts for baggy sweatpants (though I definitely understand the comfort factor!) or doesn't mind looking like I just rolled out of bed. That being said, I also know that showing up in a dress and heels will make for an uncomfortable—and chilly!—flight. So after years of trying different clothing combinations, I found these outfits to be the right combination of fashionable and functional for travel days.

CASUAL AIRPORT LOOK

When I can prioritize comfort, I wear a cute T-shirt, a nice hoodie or comfortable jacket, and Lululemon fitted pants with a tapered leg. To keep a casual outfit looking sharp, I opt for tailored-looking pieces of leisure wear and avoid athletic clothing. Casual pieces like T-shirts and hooded sweatshirts look chic and fashionable if they are made of high-quality fabrics that have a nice finish and can survive travel.

Candace's Tips and Tricks:

When it comes to making sweatpants look nice, it's all about finding fitted pieces. Anything too baggy immediately runs the risk of looking sloppy, messy, or like pajamas.

DRESSED-UP AIRPORT LOOK

For travel days when I want to look a little nicer, I typically wear a patterned wrap sweater over a plain T-shirt with half boots, an oversized scarf that doubles as a blanket for the plane, and jeans. For travel days, I like to wear jeans with Lycra in them because they have more stretch and are better for blood circulation at higher altitudes, or I opt for a non-Lycra pair with a roomy boyfriend fit. Anything too constricting and tight, like skinny jeans, should be avoided. I also have a flexible hat made by Bailey that I refer to as my "travel hat." It's perfect for flights because it can be rolled without losing its shape. Then I can throw it on after the plane lands so I don't have to worry about my hair. Cute and functional!

Carry-on Essentials for Long Flights

S'WELL WATER BOTTLE
(filled up after I go through security)

LIP BALM

GUM
*(helps with ear pressure when taking
off and landing and to refresh my breath)*

FACIAL MOISTURIZER WITH SPF
(two products in one for travel)

POUCH OF MAKEUP ESSENTIALS

PROTEIN BARS

PEN AND NOTEBOOK

CURRENT DEVOTIONAL

BOOK

LAPTOP COMPUTER

**NOISE-CANCELING
HEADPHONES**

ARRIVING AT THE DESTINATION!

Every single time my plane lands, I immediately feel a rush of excitement. I love arriving in a new place! I love going to my hotel and getting everything set up for the days ahead. I always unpack my clothes immediately. I hang dresses and fold pants and T-shirts. Unpacking clothes really helps to maintain quality pieces so they last for years. It also makes it much easier and more enjoyable to get dressed. Nobody likes scrambling through a suitcase (no matter how organized it may be).

PART TWO

Skin Care, Makeup & Hair Care

An adjective I hear all the time when it comes to looking really healthy and beautiful is *glowing*. When a woman is pregnant, when someone falls in love, when humans experience moments of pride and happiness, they all exude radiance. We say they *glow*. I love the connotation because it perfectly captures the idea that beauty emanates from within. It emphasizes beauty as not just a physical state but a spiritual one too.

As a celebrity I am especially aware that how I look is a message to the world. People often ask me about my skin-care and makeup routines. They want to know how I achieve a look that is as natural as it is "glowy." I almost always answer that it's really about skin care. Few of us are blessed with flawless skin without the effort of taking care of it by using quality products, eating well, and staying hydrated.

In order for makeup to look good, you need to start with a base layer of clear and healthy skin. Any celebrity makeup artist will tell you that when he or she is working on someone, much of the time is spent prepping the skin. But even that helps only if you've been diligent to tend to it all the days in between.

In order for makeup to look good, you need to start with a base layer of clear and healthy skin.

My Skin-Care Routine

There are many wonderful tried, tested, and true products on the market. As recommended by my dermatologist, Dr. Harold Lancer, I use the 3-Step Lancer Method of Polish, Cleanse, and Nourish for my skin-care routine. However, I admit that as much as a particular skin-care system may work for me, I like to try other skin-care regimens once I've completed several months of its use. I find that putting a new skin-care line in rotation after several months breathes new life into my skin. My skin seems to get too used to the same routine year after year, which can cause products to lose their effectiveness.

MORNING SKIN CARE

I keep my morning skin-care routine as simple as possible, following these three steps.

①︎ *CLEANSE.* We all know we should wash our faces twice a day, but how often do you skip doing it? It is the most important step you can take for your skin, so don't overlook this simple process. I always take a few minutes to wash because I want the cleansing product to really soak into my skin. I like to use small, repetitive motions to massage the cleanser into my face. These motions increase the circulation in my face, helping to wake up my skin and work the cleanser deep into my pores. When I'm done, I rinse my face with warm water.

(2) *NOURISH.* Next, I apply moisturizer. Any dermatologist will tell you that moisturizing is an important part of protecting the skin's natural barrier. It's even important for people with oily skin who are prone to acne, though it sounds counterintuitive. Your skin will produce less oil if it's well moisturized. In my case, I have mostly normal skin (somewhere between dry and oily), and I love using moisturizer in the morning. My skin doesn't feel right without it. It's also a great base for makeup!

3 **PROTECT**. Finally, I add sunscreen. I know some moisturizers have SPF in them, but I've found it more helpful to add sun protection last. That way it seals in the rest of the products by sitting on top of them and giving you a protective base before you add your makeup.

Candace's Tips and Tricks:

Taking your time with your skin-care routine really pays off. It takes a few minutes for products to completely soak into the skin, so leaving a few minutes between each step can really make a difference.

THESE ARE MY *Go-to*
SKIN-CARE PRODUCTS:

LANCER THE METHOD: POLISH

LANCER THE METHOD: CLEANSE

LANCER THE METHOD: NOURISH

NEUTROGENA ULTRA SHEER
DRY-TOUCH SUNSCREEN
BROAD SPECTRUM IN SPF 55

ELIZABETH ARDEN PREVAGE
CITY SMART BROAD SPECTRUM
SPF 50 HYDRATING SHIELD

I really believe in investing in skin-care products if possible, but good budget-friendly alternatives can be found at your local drugstore. For example, Cetaphil Gentle Skin Cleanser is a great alternative that many dermatologists recommend.

NIGHTTIME SKIN CARE

At night, I'm especially thorough. After a long day, my skin always needs some extra attention.

(1) *REMOVE EYE MAKEUP.* Before I do anything, I take off my eye makeup. Every. Single. Night. Whether I've had on only a touch of mascara or a smoky eye with a full set of false eyelashes, my eyes need to rest without anything on them. My absolute favorite sensitive eye makeup remover is Epicuren's Crystal Clear. A great budget friendly option is L'Oréal's eye makeup remover.

Candace's Tips and Tricks:

As someone who suffers from cystic acne and isn't always in the same city as my dermatologist to treat it, I've found that using light technology to target acne has been really helpful! While I was shooting a film, a makeup artist introduced me to the Zeno Acne Clearing Device. It was a lifesaver when I felt a large, painful bump coming in on my chin. The Zeno stopped it from getting any larger, and the cyst dissipated within a few days, when typically, if left untreated, it can last about three weeks. I bought the device for myself, and now I never travel without it.

(2) *POLISH.* Next, I begin Dr. Lancer's 3-step system and exfoliate my skin. I stay away from products that are too abrasive (like ones with microbeads) and instead look for products that will lightly polish the skin and remove any dead skin cells.

(3) *CLEANSE.* Then I wash my face. Don't skip this step! Even though you polished your face, it's not the same as cleansing it. I love feeling like I'm taking off the day and preparing myself for a fresh start the next day. This step also really helps to keep skin healthy, since it removes any remaining makeup and dirt particles that would otherwise clog pores and cause breakouts during sleep.

(4) *NOURISH.* Moisturizers designed specifically for use at night often contain more vitamins and antioxidants than day moisturizers, and they tend to be a little thicker. This is because skin absorbs more product during sleep, so it's important to put a product with high-quality ingredients on your face. Most dermatologists recommend looking for products with hyaluronic acid for moisture or retinol for skin-cell turnover.

(5) *ADD EYE CREAM.* This is a step I definitely skipped when I was younger, but it has become so important as I've gotten older. Eye cream really helps to preserve and moisturize the thin area of skin around the eye, giving it a more youthful and awake appearance. Coconut oil can also be a great alternative.

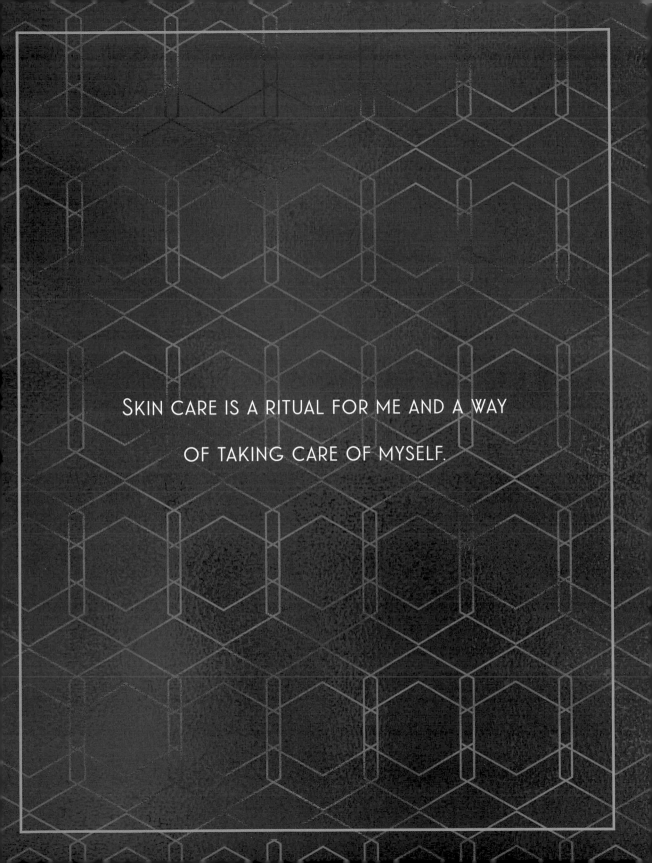

Skin care is a ritual for me and a way
of taking care of myself.

FIND WHAT WORKS FOR YOU

Skin varies from person to person, so everyone should look for products that fit their specific skin-care needs. Finding systems that really worked for me and my skin took time. Sometimes I found a product that took care of one problem but then caused another. For example, acne creams may dry up spots, but they can also over-dry areas that are otherwise healthy. It really helps to have a dermatologist who can build a system that keeps your skin healthy and glowing. Lastly, keep in mind that your needs will change with age, climate, and location. Even if something has worked in the past, don't be afraid to try new products or put them in rotation every three to six months.

Candace's Tips and Tricks:

It is important to handle the under-eye area of the skin delicately and with care, since the skin here is thinner than skin on the other parts of the face. Use a light touch to apply eye cream. Some makeup artists even suggest using your ring finger for application, since it naturally applies less force. Always pat in an upward motion, training your skin to defy gravity!

The Ultimate Polish

I have had all sorts of makeup looks created for my roles on television shows, movies, and red carpets, but my favorite everyday makeup look is a really natural one. For me, makeup is the final polish. It's a way to enhance and highlight natural features. I use makeup to even out my skin tone, brighten my complexion, and add a small touch of color for a look that is crisp, clean, and, yes, a little dewy and glowy!

My favorite everyday makeup look is a really natural one.

EYEBROWS

I always start with my eyebrows. Not only do they frame your face, but they are the most expressively used feature on you! You may have wildly thick and lush brows or thin, almost nonexistent ones like me, but either way, taking control of your brows and giving them a beautiful shape changes everything. I mainly need to fill in my eyebrows with a soft taupe color to give them a fuller appearance because they are blonde and thin. I don't dramatically reshape them, although I do make sure the shape has an arch and they are consistent.

For a natural, everyday brow, I use Benefit's Precisely, My Brow Eyebrow Pencil. Sometimes I use a taupe shadow (the Sonia Kashuk eye palette is perfect for this—see "Eye Shadow") with an angled brush. I might play with a more dramatic eyebrow shape or a deeper tone if I'm getting glammed up for the evening. Either way, I always finish off my brows with a gel to set them, such as Maybelline's Eyestudio Brow Drama Sculpting Brow Mascara or Benefit's 3D BROWtones Eyebrow Enhancer.

EYE SHADOW

When I'm doing my own makeup, I do my eye shadow before applying foundation. This is in part because if I mess it up, it's easy to take it off and start over! It also means that I can use makeup remover to wipe off any color that might fall onto my cheeks or chin without worrying about messing up my foundation and concealer. I like a little leeway for mistakes!

I put on eye-shadow primer before I apply any color so that the eye makeup will last all day. Then I choose eye shadows in subtle colors like light pinks and browns. By putting a darker shade in the crease and a lighter color on the lid, I can achieve a little dimension while also keeping that really soft and natural look. Since I have blue eyes, I also like to stick to classic colors that complement them, like taupes and rusty peaches.

You can find my favorite budget-friendly palette at Target by Sonia Kashuk: Eye Couture Eye Palette in Eye on Neutral 02. My splurge-worthy palette is Hourglass Modernist Eyeshadow Palette in Infinity.

CONCEALER

Once my eye shadow is done, I add concealer. Some people start with color correctors in peach to cover dark under-eye circles or green to cancel out redness in skin. For me, I mostly use concealer to cover dark sun spots on my face and to brighten under my eyes. With all the work and travel I do, concealer definitely comes in handy! I use a stick concealer, like Bobbi Brown Face Touch Up Stick or Clé de Peau Beauté Concealer.

Candace's Tips and Tricks:

I keep two to three different shades of concealer on hand
so, depending on my tan, I can blend them to create the perfect color.
I usually just use the back of my hand to do the blending and
apply with my ring finger.

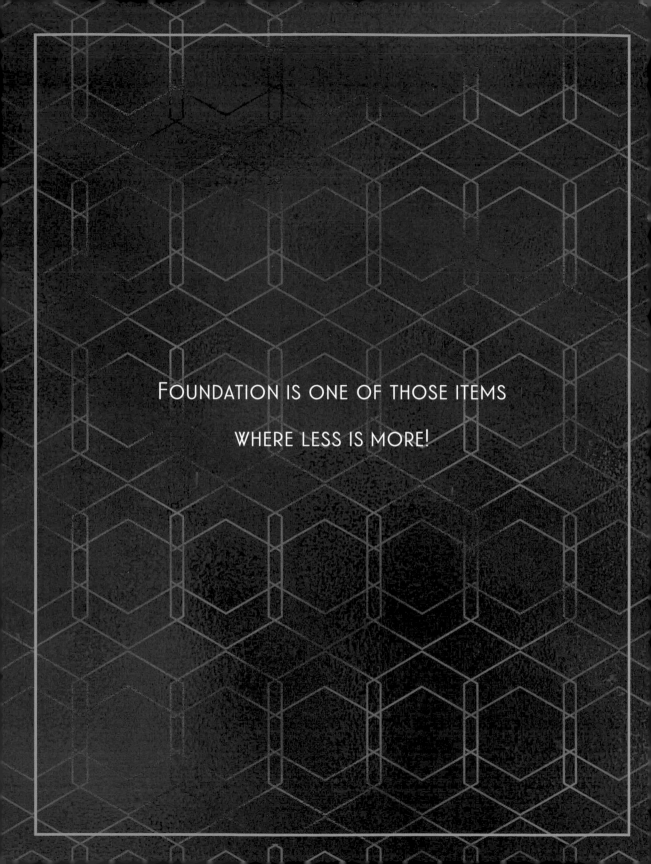

FOUNDATION IS ONE OF THOSE ITEMS

WHERE LESS IS MORE!

FOUNDATION

When the concealer is finished settling into my skin, I add foundation. I usually only use a drop or two of foundation, which I blend into my skin using a brush or a sponge. Foundation is one of those items where less is more! If skin is properly moisturized, then the foundation should spread easily and give your skin a smooth and even appearance. Some freckles and other marks might peek through foundation, but I think that's the way it should be! Our faces look much more natural when foundation is a thin layer that evens everything out rather than a heavy layer that covers everything up.

In my real life and on camera, I most often use Giorgio Armani's Luminous Silk Foundation or Make Up For Ever's Ultra HD Foundation. A great drugstore option that works well in the humidity is Revlon's ColorStay Makeup. For a barely there foundation, try Elizabeth Arden's Prevage Anti-Aging Foundation with SPF 30. The texture is so smooth and light.

CONTOUR AND BRONZER

Once my complexion is all even, I add shape to my face by contouring. I like to contour with a soft bronzer that I put on the hollows beneath my cheeks, down the sides of my nose, and on my chin and forehead (all the places the sun would darken naturally). I don't like really dramatic lines, so I try to blend in the contour shade so it looks blurry and soft. The best natural-looking one I've found is Benefit's Hoola Bronzer.

BLUSH

I love blush! I use both powder and cream, depending on the day. If I want a more dewy, natural look, I opt for cream blush. One Over One has great options—any of their duo tones will work well and make for a very natural, flushed looking cheek.

When I'm working or I have a full day, I use powder blush, which tends to stay on longer. My favorite ones are by NARS in the shades Torrid and Desire. When my skin feels dry, I'll use a cream blush right after applying my foundation and follow it up with a powder blush on top. Blush instantly makes you look awake and refreshed! It makes all the difference.

EYELINER

If I'm doing a simple daytime look, then I will wear eyeliner only on the top lash line and usually use an eye shadow rather than a pencil so it looks soft. I try to draw or smudge the line as close to my natural lash line as possible so it just enhances what's already there and makes my eyes pop. When I want a more defined line, I use a long-lasting gel eyeliner like one from Bobbi Brown or MAC Cosmetics.

MASCARA

If I could have only one makeup essential, it would be mascara—I'm totally obsessed! I always curl my eyelashes first to give them a longer appearance. No matter who's doing my makeup, I always do my own mascara. I take my time, coating each and every one of my precious lashes from the base to the tip.

The best curlers in my opinion are by Shu Uemura, Bobbi Brown, and Tweezerman. My favorite mascaras are L'Oréal's Voluminous and Benefit's They're Real.

Candace's Tips and Tricks:

Don't be afraid to layer your mascaras and even alternate between two kinds. I switch between dark brown for a really natural look and black for more definition. I also wear waterproof so it lasts throughout the day.

LIPSTICK

For my day-to-day look, I opt for a soft pink or nude color that's pretty close to the natural color of my lips. No matter what color I change my hair to—my natural dirty blonde, strawberry blonde, or deep auburn red, I can still wear these neutral shades. My go-tos are Bobbi Brown's Pale Pink, Lipstick Queen's Saint Bare Nude, or a lip oil in any color by One Over One.

I also love a bold red lip—it's so classic and pretty! I wear it any time of the year, and at any time of day. For an eye-popping red, try CoverGirl's Colorlicious Lipstick in Garnet Flame, or fill in your lips with Inglot's AMC Lip Pencil in #21 and top with clear gloss.

FINISHED LOOK

When I'm done, I set my look with a dusting of pressed powder. It seals your foundation and reduces shine, sending you off looking totally calm, collected, and cool!

*When It Comes to Your Hair,
Be Brave!*

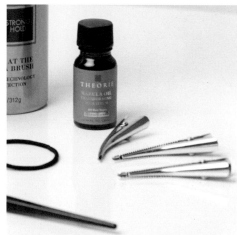

It's no secret that I like to change my hair. I've been a blonde, a brunette, and a redhead. I've tried pretty much every length out there—from short bobs to long, layered cuts. People often ask me how I can be so brave about my hair. The truth is, I know it grows back! No style is permanent, and I think there is something transformative and powerful about a haircut. Like any change, it can bring out other sides of my personality.

I also alternate between long and short styles to keep my hair healthy. Whenever my hair has been long for a while and it's been colored for different roles, there comes a point when I need to cut it to maintain its health. That's part of the reason why I've had so many different hairstyles over the years!

These days I'm back to loose blonde waves for *Fuller House*. People ask me all the time how my hair is done on the show. I especially get a lot of questions about how to do my signature ponytail, so I've included a full tutorial. Hello, D. J. Tanner (Fuller)!

BEACHY WAVES

In order to do my ponytail, I first style my hair in loose beachy waves. It gives texture and body that will make your ponytail pop. And mastering this technique lays the groundwork for many beautiful hairstyles.

(1) I start by blow-drying my hair to give it body. You should make sure the dryer blows your hair in the opposite direction of how it grows naturally in order to really add some volume. I also like using a round brush to make the effect more dramatic.

Candace's Tips and Tricks:

Sectioning the hair is very important when styling! I keep my sections clean and secured by using large clips. Plastic chopsticks are also efficient.

(2) I use a graduated (tapered) curling wand for my waves. I curl the hair from my ears forward away from my face, then curl the rest in alternating directions to give my hair that true beachy effect. I wrap each piece around the wand for 4 to 5 seconds and then let it cool without separating the wave (that part comes later). I find curling wands to be much easier to handle than curling irons, and it makes the process go much faster!

(3) Using a texturizing spray (Oribe is my favorite), I simultaneously break up the waves with my fingers and add the product for maximum volume and an undone, tousled texture.

(4) I finish all of my styles with Kérastase Laque Couture Medium Hold Hairspray. I love how touchable my hair feels, and the hold lasts all day. My favorite drugstore hairspray is L'Oréal's Elnett Satin Strong Hold.

Now my beachy waves are set and ready!

Candace's Tips and Tricks:

Adding oil, like The Hair Oil by Prim Botanicals, will keep your hair looking incredibly healthy and shiny without any greasy residue. I recommend applying two to three pumps of this oil from the mid-strand to the ends, avoiding the root area if desired, especially if you have a finer hair texture like me. I rub the oil on the front and back of my hands like a lotion and then run my fingers through my hair for even application.

MY SIGNATURE PONYTAIL

I wear this ponytail all the time, and it works especially well on second-day hair. So what I usually like to do is style my hair in beachy waves the day that I wash it, then pull it up in this ponytail the next day. Two hairstyles for the effort of one!

(1) Section off hair horizontally across the top of your head from ear to ear, creating two parts.

(2) Tease the back portion of your hair at the crown with a comb so that it creates a bump for height. Take the front portion of your hair and smooth it over the top of the crown.

(3) Pull up hair and secure it with an elastic band. For maximum volume at the crown, pull the now-secured elastic out about an inch and re-cinch the pony.

(4) Pull out a piece of hair to wrap around the hairband so that it doesn't show. Secure it with a bobby pin. This last step really adds a polished touch!

Candace's Tips and Tricks:

For a more effortless, lived-in look, pull out a few pieces around the face, or leave bangs down if you have them. A comb can also be used to take pieces of hair out of your ponytail. Just place the sharp end of the comb on the section you want to pull out, weave the end in, and gently pull. Hold your ponytail while you do this to help keep it intact.

My Hairstyles Through the Years

How to Minimize Hair Damage

Since I color and heat-style my hair so often, I have to take steps to minimize hair damage. As I mentioned before, I cut my hair between roles to keep it healthy. I also typically wash my hair only every other day, and when I do, I use shampoo and conditioner for color-treated hair, like Kevin.Murphy's Angel.Wash and Angel.Rinse. I give my hair a break on days when I'm not filming by letting it air-dry (I try to do this at least once or twice a week). And last but not least, I put essential oils in my hair while I sleep. I add rosemary oil to my scalp before bed because it helps with growth and smells so good! If your hair tends to get oily quickly and you don't want to add oil near the roots, then I'd suggest a spray that can dispense a small amount of essential oils. Sprays tend to be much lighter, and even one to two spritzes can really help the health of your hair!

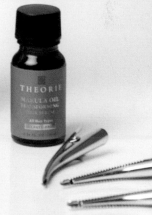

There is something transformative
and powerful about a haircut.
Like any change, it can bring out
other sides of your personality.

PART THREE

Health, Fitness &
Nourishing Your Spirit

Even though this is the last section in this book, in my opinion, it's by far the most important. Living a healthy life is the first step to appearing strong, beautiful, and happy. In this fast-paced world, personal well-being can be one of the hardest things to prioritize. As a wife and mom, I have a natural impulse to put my family first. As an actress who always wants to be challenged and grow in my career, I find it's also easy to put work first. As a friend, I know that I want to be the kind of person who will always be there for the people close to me. So I've had points in my life when I put myself and my needs last. It wasn't until I realized that taking care of myself would make me better at taking care of other people that I was really able to shift my priorities and put my health and wellness at the top of my priority list.

I want to honor the body God gave me, and I believe that taking care of myself mentally, spiritually, and physically is a way of loving and glorifying Him. These are the practices that really help me stay balanced, healthy, and whole.

Living a healthy life is the first step to appearing strong, beautiful, and happy.

Feel-Good Foods

I don't think it's a mystery why the Bible mentions food so many times. Food is at the center of our lives! It's an important cultural and social practice. Preparing and eating food brings us together as families, neighbors, and friends. It's also what nourishes us, providing us with vitamins, minerals, and the much-needed calories that fuel our bodies. What we eat contributes to how much energy we have, how long we live, and how *well* we live.

I haven't always had the best relationship with food. There was a time in my life when I struggled emotionally and used food as my comfort instead of turning to God's grace. I've also struggled over the years with what to eat and how much to eat. That's why I am so grateful to have reached a place where I can enjoy and embrace food in the ways I believe God intended. At this point in my life, I've learned what foods my body responds to best and am continually refining that list as my body grows older and changes. I know that eating well makes me feel good on the inside, and that shows on the outside.

Eating well makes me feel good on the inside, and that shows on the outside.

These are some of the recipes, tips, and tricks that have helped me to embrace a well-balanced and nutritious life.

HEALTHY SNACKS

A major part of eating well is having healthy snacks around that are easy to grab when you are on the go. People typically make unhealthy choices when they are busy and don't feel like they have time to find healthy food. So they grab whatever is around them instead of seeking out more nutritious options. It wasn't until I learned how easy, convenient, and beneficial it was to keep healthy snacks around that my diet really changed for the better.

Eating well doesn't have to be time-consuming, and it doesn't have to cost a fortune!

Candace's Tips and Tricks:

It can help to make your own snack packs at the beginning of the week by placing these items into reusable containers. I also like to wash and cut certain fruits and vegetables into bite-size pieces so they are cleaned, prepped, and ready to go.

A FEW OF MY *favorite* SNACKS:

NUGO SLIM VEGAN PROTEIN BARS

NUGO NUTRITION FIBER D'LISH BARS

FRESH, WHOLE FRUIT
*like oranges, tangerines, apples, bananas, mangoes, pineapples,
kiwis, berries, and seasonal fruit*

HUMMUS WITH FRESH-CUT FRUITS AND VEGGIES
*like cauliflower, broccoli, snap peas, celery, carrots,
bell peppers, and grape tomatoes*

A SMALL HANDFUL OF RAW, UNSALTED NUTS
I prefer pistachios, almonds, and cashews

A HARD-BOILED EGG OR EGG WHITES
I like them with sriracha hot sauce for a little kick!

SMALL BAKED SWEET POTATO OR YAM

STARKIST TUNA AND SALMON CREATIONS POUCHES
These are great for on the go!

WASA OR KAVLI CRISPBREAD CRACKERS
with a tablespoon of guacamole or peanut butter

EASY MEALS

I am not the cook of the house! If I do make something, it needs to be extremely easy with few ingredients. My husband, Val, does most the heavy lifting in this department. Because of my lack of cooking experience early in our marriage and his need for three hot meals a day for his hockey career, he took over the responsibility. Over the years, Val became passionate about cooking and food and is now an excellent chef. I couldn't even begin to make the kinds of delicious dishes he does, so I don't. Instead, I make reservations! However, I do have a few quick-and-easy meals that I like to make in a pinch that don't require much cooking.

WHOLE-WHEAT PITA POCKET WITH TUNA SALAD. I make the tuna salad with light mayo or reduced-fat Vegenaise, and then I pack the pita with lettuce, sprouts, onion, tomato, and carrots.

HUMMUS VEGGIE WRAP. I spread two tablespoons of hummus on one whole-wheat tortilla and add sliced veggies such as arugula, carrots, cucumbers, bell peppers, onion, tomato, baby spinach, and cabbage.

QUINOA SALAD. To make this salad, I pair 1 cup of cooked quinoa with cooked arugula, kale, broccoli florets, and yellow and red tomatoes.

VEGGIE PATTY WRAPPED IN LETTUCE. I almost always eat this with either mustard or hot sauce. Adding a condiment really gives this meal the right amount of kick! I'll also add onion, tomato, and avocado.

EVERYTHING IN MODERATION

I really don't like to think of food in terms of restrictions, like what to avoid. I think everything in moderation can be fine. I mean, I would

never want to give up carrot cake forever! However, I have learned that certain foods don't make me feel as good and don't fuel my body so that it runs at its peak condition. So in general, I try to stay away from dairy, red meat, refined sugar, white flour, and processed foods, or I eat them in very limited quantities. Staying away from dairy has had the biggest effect on my body. I no longer have a nagging, phlegm-filled cough, my face isn't puffy, my sinuses aren't congested, and I get fewer pimples. I'm convinced that sugar is a drug as much as caffeine or any prescription drug is. It's addictive, and my body craves it when I eat even the smallest amounts. It becomes a cycle of sugar highs and sugar crashes, so I find it best to steer clear of it so my body feels consistently energized from natural sources.

What I eat most often are vegetables, fruits, whole grains, legumes, beans, nuts, seeds, fish and seafood, eggs, herbs, and olive oil. I don't know that there is an actual name for how I eat . . . Mediterranean? Mostly vegan plus fish? Pescatarian, no dairy? Call it whatever you want; I just listen to what my body responds to best and have trained it to enjoy and crave those foods, even if I didn't at the start.

STAYING HYDRATED

Water is one of the most important elements we can put in our bodies. It helps every system and cell inside the body function. Remember, the average adult body contains 60 percent water and needs to be replenished! To ensure you drink enough daily, search online for a hydration calculator to find out how much you need each day based on your height, weight, gender, and activity level. I carry my 25-ounce S'well bottle everywhere I go and know that I must drink three to four full bottles each day to properly hydrate. Remember, just as plants and flowers bloom when they're given water and light, so does your body!

Candace's Tips and Tricks:

Marilu Henner (my favorite TV mom, costar, and health advocate) convinced me to start every morning with a mixture of 1 to 2 tablespoons of Bragg Organic Apple Cider Vinegar, ¼ teaspoon of raw honey, and ½ cup of warm water. I've been drinking this for several years and am sold! The benefits are incredible, my digestion and cholesterol have improved, and it's increased my metabolism.

I carry my 25-ounce S'well bottle everywhere I go and know that I must drink three to four full bottles each day to properly hydrate.

Strengthen Your Body

Fitness has become such a major part of my life as I've gotten older. At 41, I now fully understand the physical, mental, and even spiritual benefits of strengthening my body through exercise. I feel whole, complete, powerful, and inspired when I work out. I also know that this is a step I have to take in order to be the best wife and mother I can be. If I want to live a long and fulfilling life with my husband and kids, then I have to focus on my health and make it a priority.

If I want to live a long and fulfilling life with my husband and kids, then I have to focus on my health and make it a priority.

I also love how strong working out makes me feel. Physical changes can trigger mental changes too! I've found that I take more initiative when I work out. I feel mighty and confident. I've also found that I have more to give to others because I feel stronger and more capable. It really is the gift that keeps on giving.

At this point, I always try to fit in some kind of workout every day. Sometimes I will have a full hour to do exercises either alone or with my trainer, Kira Stokes, in person, via FaceTime, or by watching her online videos. Sometimes I will have only 10 minutes . . . and I still use the 10 minutes. With exercise it's true that every little bit helps! Here are a few of my favorite moves from The Stoked Method by Kira Stokes.

REVERSE LUNGE/SHOULDER PRESS

Focus muscle groups: glutes, quads, shoulders, core

(1) With weight on your left heel and a dumbbell over your right shoulder, extend your right leg back to bring your right knee 1 inch from the ground. Both knees should form 90-degree angles when in lunge position, and keep your core strong.

② Drive from your left heel to return to a standing balance, and perform one shoulder press to extend your arm by your ear. Be sure to squeeze your left glute as you perform this movement.

③ Continue for 12 reps; then switch legs. Do 3 sets of 12. Choose a weight that's challenging but doable with proper form (I use 8 to 10 pounds).

Candace's Tips and Tricks:

Driving from your heels when working the lower body helps initiate glute engagement and focus—something we all need and want. If you push from the balls of your feet, you focus more on your quads. Ninety percent of us are quad-dominant, and we tend to sit often (I call it the "sit and spread") so . . . let's get those glutes fired up!

ONE-LEGGED DEADLIFT/BICEPS CURL

Focus muscle groups: glutes, hamstrings, biceps, core

(1) With weights in each hand and balancing on your right leg with your right knee soft (bent slightly), hinge forward from your hips with a flat back and lift your left leg behind you. Your upper body and left leg should move at the same rate (like a seesaw), keeping your core engaged and strong.

(2) When your upper body and leg reach a parallel position to the floor (depending on your hamstring flexibility), return to your starting position and perform one biceps curl with both arms. Be sure to squeeze your right glute as you perform this movement.

(3) Continue for 12 reps; then switch legs. Do 3 sets of 12. Choose a weight that is challenging but doable while maintaining proper form (I use 8 to 10 pounds).

Candace's Tips and Tricks:

Proper form is essential to an effective workout and helps prevent injury. Work hard to keep your hips square throughout this movement. (It's a great idea to try all strength moves without weights first so you can understand the movement and be confident in your form.)

LATERAL LUNGE/LATERAL RAISE

Focus muscle groups: inner/outer thighs, glutes, shoulders, core

(1) Step out laterally (to the side) with your right leg, and sit back into your right hip with weight on your right heel and your knee aligned over your foot. Your right hip, knee, and ankle should aligned, with both feet pointing forward, both kneecaps pointing forward. Hold one weight inside your legs and one outside.

(2) Driving from your right heel, return to a standing position with weights by your sides. Perform one lateral raise to bring the weights to shoulder height, keeping a slight bend in your elbows.

(3) Perform in the same manner, stepping out to the left. Continue alternating for 8 to 10 reps on each side. Choose a weight that's challenging but doable while maintaining proper form (I use 5 to 8 pounds).

TRICEPS PUSH-UPS

Focus muscle groups: triceps, shoulders, core

(1) Start in an extended arm plank, with your shoulders directly over your wrists, your navel pulled toward your spine, and your glutes engaged.

(2) Rotate the creases of your elbows forward and shift your shoulders over your wrists slightly.

(3) Bend your elbows to lower your shoulders to elbow height. Your elbows should skim the sides of your body and hug your rib cage.

(4) Press back up to your starting position and continue 12 to 15 reps. Focus on quality over quantity. Modify and drop to your knees at any point if you need to in order to keep your form correct.

Candace's Tips and Tricks:

A push-up is a moving plank, so your core is very involved. Remember to squeeze your butt cheeks like you have a check for a million dollars between them and you have to hold it there, and draw your navel toward your spine. Your body should move as one unit as you lower and lift.

RENEGADE ROW/KICKBACK

Focus muscle groups: back, triceps, shoulders, core

(1) Start in a plank position with hands on weights, feet slightly wider than hip width.

(2) Perform a lateral row where your elbow skims the side of your body. Once your elbow is by your side, straighten the arm to perform a triceps kickback.

(3) Reverse the movement to return to a plank position, and repeat on the other side.

(4) Continue alternating for 12 reps each side. Choose a weight that's challenging but doable (I use 10 to 12 pounds).

Candace's Tips and Tricks:

Adding a playful element to workouts is always a bonus. Whether it's taking a moment to "dance it out," rock a cartwheel, or kick up to a handstand, finding movements that make your soul sing makes every workout more fun. Any kind of inversion (headstand, handstand, and so forth) brings blood to the brain, which is extremely energizing, so . . . get upside down!

SIDE PLANK

Focus muscle groups: core, shoulders

(1) Start in an extended arm plank, shoulders directly over wrists, navel to spine, glutes engaged.

(2) Walk your right hand to the midline of your body and roll onto the outside edge of your right foot; your right shoulder and wrist should be in alignment. Extend your left arm toward the ceiling and continue to reach.

(3) Be sure to drive your hips up, maintaining a slight tuck to the tailbone (glutes engaged).

(4) Hold for 30 seconds and then repeat on the left. Do 3 sets on alternating sides.

Candace's Tips and Tricks:

Your core is the powerhouse of your body. Connecting with it during all movements is key to developing the proper foundation to move, stabilize, and develop strength properly.

I LOVE HOW STRONG WORKING OUT

MAKES ME FEEL.

JUMPING ROPE

Jumping rope is a great way to get your heart rate up to a challenging level, and it's super portable—a jump rope can travel anywhere. Try jumping rope in between strength circuits to get more bang for your buck. And remember, practice makes perfect. You probably won't be Rocky your first time out of the gate, but don't get discouraged. With a little patience and perseverance, you'll be nailing double-unders in no time.

FUN FACT: A minute of jumping rope where you clear the rope 80 times a minute is like running an 8-minute mile. Major calorie burner!

A minute of jumping rope where you clear the rope eighty times a minute is like running an 8-minute mile.

Nourishing Your Spirit

Eating well and exercising are really important for your well-being, but nourishing your spirit is even more important. There is nothing that will better prepare you to understand your purpose, navigate the twists and turns of life, stay strong during difficult and traumatic events, and even celebrate the happy and blessed moments than being grounded in your faith. I know that the foundation of who I am in every aspect of my life rests in my relationship with Jesus Christ. I am a daughter of the King, created and woven together by God the Father Himself. I know this to be true because I read the Bible and believe it is the inspired and infallible Word of God. Knowing God is truly the most important part of my life because it doesn't end on this earth. We will all spend eternity somewhere, and I want to spend it with the Lord, Jesus Christ. That is why I prioritize time for my relationship with Jesus through Bible study, church, and prayer.

Nourishing your spirit is easy to do, but just like eating well and exercising, it requires intention. Take time each day to put your life into perspective by focusing on your relationship with God. There are ways to ground yourself every day, and these are the ones that work for me.

Nourishing your spirit is easy to do, but just like eating well and exercising, it requires intention.

PRAYER

I couldn't imagine a day going by without starting it off in prayer. You see, I hadn't always done it, so I've seen how much it changed my life when I started focusing on prayer in my late twenties. Talking to God not only prepares me for the day by filling up my spirit with the Holy Spirit, but protects me with the armor of truth that I put on verbally and guides me to live with the fruits of the Spirit—love, joy, peace, patience, kindness, goodness, faithfulness, gentleness, and self-control—as I encounter people throughout my day. I know, that may sound like mumbo jumbo if you haven't read the Bible before, but these things are given to us as we cultivate a life with Jesus.

There are days when I know exactly what I need help and guidance with, and I pray specifically about those things. And there are also times when I don't know what I need, what I want, or where I should be headed. I also pray specifically about those things, praying for God's will, not my own, and that He'll show me by opening and closing doors through relationships, job opportunities, or specific paths I may be traveling down. It's important for me to share with you that I don't take it all in as a universal guidance of coincidence, happenstance, karma, or luck, but I line up what I'm feeling, seeing, or hearing with the Word of God so that I know it's actually direction from God. I hope that makes sense, and if not, check out my website, candacecameronbure.net, for more information on how to get to know God.

Prayer also brings me peace and clarity that I can't find on my own. When I pray, I talk to God about everything: moments that happened during the day, hopes for my family, fears I'm trying to overcome, or doubts I have about something I'm trying to accomplish. There isn't anything too big or too small to talk to God about. And trust me, when you pray specifically, you'll see your prayers answered. It may not always be in the way you expected, but they will get answered. God is always waiting for you, listening to you, and there for you. You are never alone, and you are loved by Him.

Prayer brings me a peace and clarity that I can't find on my own.

WRITING IN A JOURNAL

Writing in a journal helps me unload. This can be a form of prayer too. I can write down my worries, hopes, memories, and dreams. It gives me a way to check in with myself and to reflect on the thoughts that are floating around in my head. It can also help me identify patterns of behavior, measure my growth in different areas, and reflect on my goals for the future.

I also think journaling can be a great tool for setting priorities. Some journals, like bullet journals, have specific systems for creating to-do lists that help keep people on task. When there is so much going on in life, it can be beneficial to write down a plan for how you want to tackle each day. It ensures that days are organized by what you want to be achieving instead of by default habits and patterns.

Journaling helps you be intentional about your thoughts and prayer life.

I also use a bullet-point system for my big prayer requests that may take time to see come to fruition. Some of mine have included writing a book (check!), starring in a new family-friendly television show (check!), and cohosting a daytime talk show (check!). It's incredible to be able to look back after years of praying for something and be able to write a check mark with a date next to it to remind myself of when God answered that prayer. Other big prayers may be buying or selling your home, finding a new job, choosing the right school for your child, repairing a relationship

with your spouse, or praying for a friend's salvation. Journaling helps you be intentional about your thoughts and prayer life.

Candace's Tips and Tricks:

Journaling may seem like a daunting undertaking, but it doesn't have to be! Taking even a few minutes at the end of the day to jot down what you're most grateful for or even write down your prayer requests is a great way to begin the practice of journaling.

READING

I love to read! No matter what I'm going through or what challenges I'm facing, I know that reading can take my mind off my immediate surroundings and give me a fresh perspective on life. It's one of the best ways to see the world from someone else's point of view. It introduces me to new ways of thinking and different ways of living so I can understand where someone may be coming from. It helps me learn about distant cultures and places I've never been. It makes me feel more connected to the world and other people. The power of a great book is that it brings people together.

*The power of a great book is that
it brings people together.*

This is also why I love reading with my kids! Reading is a way to teach them values and lessons and to bond with them as they grow up. Sometimes a story can be a really easy way to talk about difficult subjects like bullying or not fitting in. Sometimes it's just a way to have fun as a family. So many nights I'd gather my kids on the couch or in my bed and I'd read them stories in different accents and funny voices. I loved hearing their giggles, I loved seeing their faces light up at the illustrations, and most of all, I loved the conversations we'd have afterwards about what they learned or how the story made them feel.

As my kids have grown older, reading together has helped us stay close. We read devotionals together, or I'll read the books they're reading concurrently so we can talk about our ideas, thoughts, likes, and differences. We know that no matter what, we will understand, respect, and love one another. We know that our different voices, opinions, and points of view make us strong as a whole. Reading together makes us stronger as a family.

As my kids have grown older, reading together has helped us stay close.

I also know that I wouldn't be the person I am today if I didn't read. There are so many books that I've connected with and that have made a big impact on my life. There are books that helped me get through hard times and books that inspired me to live my life differently. I also love that different types of books serve different purposes. There are easy reads that just help me escape. There are business books that help me refocus my energy and take on problems with a fresh outlook. There are nonfiction books that inspire me to grow as a person. There are fiction books I read with the intent to turn the stories into movies. Here's a list of my favorite, absolutely-can't-miss books.

My Favorite Books

NONFICTION

GOOD FAITH, **David Kinnaman and Gabe Lyons:** What a great book about sharing your faith and beliefs about hot-topic issues without being judgmental or defensive—I couldn't have written it better myself. This book was everything I've wanted to say to the church and the body of Christ and more.

A MILLION LITTLE WAYS, **Emily P. Freeman:** This book literally helped me change the direction and course of my career. By laying down my second and third desires in life that were safe and secure, I found I could pursue my first desires in life and take a leap of faith. This book spoke to me more than any other book has at a particular time and place in my life.

THE CIRCLE MAKER, **Mark Batterson:** Prayer has changed my life, and this book encouraged me to give all my thoughts and desires to God and to be diligent to pursue Him through prayer.

THE 5 LOVE LANGUAGES, **Gary Chapman:** This has helped me and my family understand one another better. We each have a love language that speaks to us. Finding out what your family members' love languages are will help you love them in the ways they connect with. And understanding your own love language will help them love you the way you need to be loved as well.

MY UTMOST FOR HIS HIGHEST, **Oswald Chambers:** This classic devotional is still a favorite. I read it year after year.

THE HIDING PLACE, **Corrie ten Boom:** I've never read about a braver woman whose sole desire is to love God and love people.

FICTION

REDEEMING LOVE, **Francine Rivers:** The best romance book I've ever read.

THE PILGRIM'S PROGRESS, **John Bunyan:** (I prefer an updated edition in modern English.) Every Christian needs to read this book. Your children need to read this book. You need to read this book to your children. It's gripping, exciting, and powerful, and it will change your life. My choice for a children's version is *Dangerous Journey: The Story of Pilgrim's Progress* by *Oliver Henkin.*

THE HUNGER GAMES TRILOGY, **Suzanne Collins:** I read this series alongside my kids and was hooked! I read it faster than they did. The series was a great escape and better than the movies.

THE WEDDING DRESS, **Rachel Hauck:** This is a generational story about a wedding dress worn by several women. I'm a sucker for love stories, keepsakes, and tradition.

THE HELP, **Kathryn Stockette:** Even if you saw the movie, read the book. I cried; I laughed; I felt so deeply for each character.

TAKING TIME FOR YOURSELF

One of the hardest things for any mindful woman to do is to prioritize herself. We all play so many different roles: Daughter. Sister. Mom. Wife. Colleague. Friend. We all have a lot of people who depend on us, so it's easy and natural to put those people and their needs first, which isn't a bad thing! We make sure everyone and everything is set, then we promise to check in with ourselves once everything is done. News flash: everything is never done!

When I get enough rest, drink enough water, exercise, and have time to pray and invest my time with God, I am a better and stronger version of myself.

It took me a long time to realize that taking care of myself would ultimately help me take care of others. When I get enough rest, drink enough water, exercise, and have time every day to pray and invest my time with God, I am a better and stronger version of myself. I am able to give more to other people. I stop running on empty. I stop trying to juggle too many things. I find balance, and with that balance, I help other people find balance too.

It's so important to find time for yourself every day—whether that's a few quiet moments in the morning, a self-care routine that helps you feel put together, a nap, or even doing a favorite activity that revitalizes and nourishes you. Self-care looks different for everyone, and it looks different for me at different times and stages in life. On any given day, it's important to pay attention to what you need. Sometimes I know I have to exercise to feel better. Sometimes I need to go for a drive to think things through. Sometimes a coffee date with close friends is what revitalizes me. The point is, if we check in with ourselves, it can be easy to figure out what we have to do every day to take care of ourselves.

Self-care looks different for everyone, and it looks different for me at different times and stages in life.

There will still be times when we prioritize others, when we compromise between what we need and what others need. There will still be days when the most time we can find for ourselves is a few minutes here or there. But those few minutes can make a world of difference. Prioritize time for yourself, and everyone in your life will benefit.

TAKING BREAKS

Part of taking time for yourself is also knowing when it's time to take a break. It can be really hard to ask for a break. It can feel (wrongfully) like you are being lazy or selfish, but this isn't the case! Sometimes you need to put everything on pause in order to regain control of situations. Sometimes you need to rest. Sometimes you just need a few minutes to yourself. We are all human, and we can only do so much. Know when you are reaching your breaking point, and ask to take a break. It will make you feel better and more whole.

Spending Time Alone

As someone who occasionally likes to spend time alone to get back in touch with myself, I can suggest a few ideas you can do alone that might make you feel better, happier, and more inspired.

BROWSE A FARMERS' MARKET. I love going to the farmers' market with my family, but it can be a really beautiful experience alone too! Plus it allows for a lot more time to browse each vendor.

SEE A MOVIE BY YOURSELF. Movies are art to me. I love the cinematography, the character building, and the stories at the heart of each film. It can be really fun to see films with friends and family, but it can also be inspiring to go to a theater alone. Grab popcorn, and immerse yourself in a different world.

TAKE YOURSELF OUT TO DINNER. I will admit, I do this more often than I'd like to because I work out of town and on location so often, but taking yourself out to dinner, to a restaurant you love, and indulging in a meal you enjoy can be a really freeing and exhilarating experience. Add a good book, and you're really set.

WALK AROUND A CITY AND WINDOW-SHOP. I love to walk around cities alone. I love to people-watch. It's a great way to appreciate the atmospheres and personalities of different cities, whether it's Los Angeles or New York. It's also a good way to feel alone and still in other people's company at the same time.

ACTUALLY SHOP. I will happily shop with my friends and family any day of the week, but I always prefer to do it alone. It means I don't have to inconvenience anyone else if I take a little extra time in the dressing room to consider outfit options. It also means I can come home with little surprises for my hubby and kids. I'm always more efficient and productive when I shop alone.

READ IN A PARK. This is an especially great option if you live in a big city and don't get to spend a lot of time out in nature. A fresh-air break from all the concrete and hustle can be just what you need!

GO FOR A SWIM. Swimming is a great low-impact exercise that is also rejuvenating. Whether you go to a gym, a local recreational pool, or a spa close by, swimming can be a great way to enjoy some time alone.

GO FOR A RUN. Running is an equally great option! Just turn on your headphones and go.

BE CREATIVE. Color. Scrapbook. Write. Cook. It doesn't matter. When you have time to yourself, one of the best things you can do is find an outlet for exercising your creativity.

Managing Stress

The key to managing stress is giving up control. Life is not going to be perfect. Things aren't always going to happen in a way that makes sense. Part of life is chaos, so part of leading a less stressful life is accepting that chaos instead of fighting it. There are times you simply have to give your troubles to God and then let them go.

I also believe in putting every problem into perspective. Some difficulties, like death and loss, require us to grieve. But most of the stuff we spend time worrying about is small—getting a parking ticket, a problem at work, a fight with a spouse, a personal failure. In these cases, it's healthy to take a look around and ask yourself if you're okay, what's going right instead of wrong, and what can be learned from the experience. I've been amazed as I've grown older that many of the things that used to consume me with worry turned out to be minimal problems that passed with time. I wish I had been happier in those moments and enjoyed the other good things that were in my life at the time—things I couldn't appreciate!

I've been amazed as I've grown older that many of the things that used to consume me with worry turned out to be minimal problems that passed with time.

It also helps to find strength and support inside your community. Look to friends and family for help when you need it. No one can take on everything by him- or herself. Allow yourself to be vulnerable with the people close to you, and allow them to help you. We all have to hold each other up sometimes.

Allow yourself to be vulnerable with the people close to you, and allow them to help you.

This same line of thinking can be applied at work. I used to be one of those people who took on too much. If something needed to get done, I would jump right in. I didn't like to ask anyone for help—partially because I didn't want to burden anyone else, and partially because I wanted the peace of mind that everything was taken care of properly. I ended up running myself into the ground. No one person can do it all. Even at work, there is strength in the numbers. Delegating can be a really great tool. Divide up tasks and appreciate other people's strengths. Working with your community can make for a much happier (and more exciting!) workplace.

Last but not least, a key to handling stress is prioritizing. Prioritize the things that are actually important to you: your family, your friends, your work and purpose, your faith, your health. Time is limited, so we all have to be mindful about how we spend our days. My priorities are God, my family, my health, and my work. I spend a significant amount of time on those things every single day. I have learned to say no to so many other

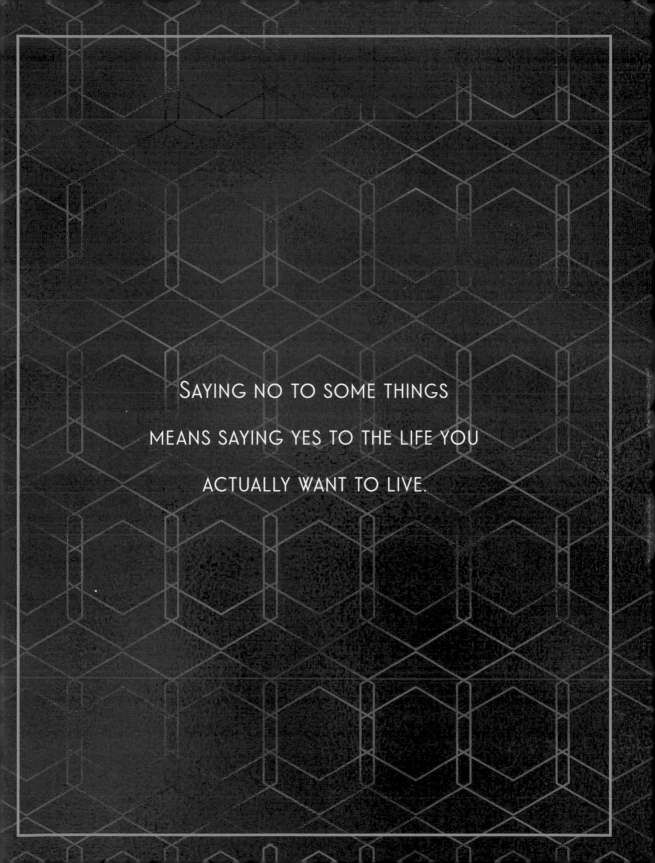

SAYING NO TO SOME THINGS
MEANS SAYING YES TO THE LIFE YOU
ACTUALLY WANT TO LIVE.

things—jobs I don't have time to take on, events I don't want to attend, and relationships that are toxic. Saying no to some things means saying yes to the life you actually want to live. There should be no fear, shame, or apology in saying no. Your life is your choice.

BEING GRATEFUL

Gratitude is a practice. Take a hard look at your surroundings. At first you may notice the things your brain has trained you to notice. There's a mess in the kitchen that needs to be picked up. There's a meeting to get to and laundry to do. Try to turn off this automatic approach that wants to get things done but too often stops you from appreciating what's right in front of you. Maybe the mess in the kitchen is your son making a sandwich for himself. The meeting is taking place because something new and exciting is happening at work. The laundry is dirty because there's been a week full of beautiful experiences—soccer games, birthday parties, family days in the park, or time spent with friends. Life is a beautiful gift, and we all have to remind ourselves to receive that gift. Practicing gratitude is the way to do that.

Life is a beautiful gift, and we all have to remind ourselves to receive that gift.

SLEEP

Eight hours. I know people say six to eight hours, but if it's at all possible, try to get all eight. Sleeping is a big part of self-care. Our bodies need time to rest and repair themselves. At night, turn off your devices, resist the urge to stay up late watching movies (so hard for me!), and get some rest. To give your all, you have to *have* your all. Sleeping is a big part of that!

Candace's Tips and Tricks:

To get more sleep, it's helpful to have a relaxing bedtime ritual. Turn off your devices, resist the urge to stay up late watching movies (so hard for me!), and wind down from the day. If worries are keeping you awake, pray and give your concerns to God.

GIVING BACK TO OTHERS

It's really easy to be pulled in by our own lives, our own responsibilities, and our own problems. But it's important to take a step back from those things and truly see other people—their lives, their responsibilities, and their problems. Life is this intricate framework of people, and each of us is only one single dot in the world. In order to live life in a full and meaningful way, we have to help others. We have to help the environment. Not only is it a responsibility; it's also rewarding. Giving back makes us feel more connected. It helps us see the larger picture. It makes it easier to put our own lives into perspective when we embrace the other lives around us. It makes us healthier, happier, and more fulfilled and whole.

As You Stay Stylish . . .

I hope you find yourself coming back to this book often, daily even, for inspiration and for the reminder that staying stylish doesn't have be overwhelming or difficult. It should be fun and celebrated—because who you see on the outside should simply be a reflection of who you are on the inside. You are unique. There is no one like you, so . . .

Just. Be. You.

Cultivate who you already are by filling your soul with goodness spiritually, nutritionally, and physically, and allow yourself to be pliable so that you can ultimately grow into the person God made you to be. A soft and loving heart, a gentle smile, compassionate eyes, and a listening ear will always outshine anything you wear.

And when you need a little motivation, inspiration, insight, vision, or creativity, flip through these pages over and over again. I know they'll help you feel certain that your outfit is on point, flatters your figure, and makes you feel comfortable so you can confidently walk out the door and embrace your life and your loved ones.

I also hope this book sparks your own original ideas. And if my fashion sense isn't necessarily your thing, keep an eye on the person's style you like most. That's how I started! As Charles Caleb Colton said, "Imitation is the sincerest [form] of flattery."

I won't mind one bit if you copy my style. ☺

Cheers!

Candace

Acknowledgments

A huge thank-you to Redrock Entertainment Development for literally managing my life. Jeffery Brooks and Ford Englerth, I couldn't do it without you.

If it weren't for the help of my personal team, both in front of the cameras and behind the scenes, I would probably run around looking like a chicken with its head cut off. Not only do you elevate my style on the red carpet and help me look my best for every interview and television project I work on, but you ground me in the midst of the chaos. Thank you, Tara Brooks, Daniel Blaylock, Joseph Cassell, and Erin MacDonald, for your expertise in makeup, hair, and style.

Melissa Coulier, I had been waiting for the right "big thing" to work on with you, and the moment a style book was decided on, I knew this was it! Thank you for capturing the real me so brilliantly through your photography.

Thank you to the team at Zondervan—Dawn Hollomon, Adam Hill, Molly Hodgin, Jennifer Gott, Karissa Taylor, Jennifer Greenwalt, Carly Kellerman, Michael Aulisio, Tim Marshall, Mandy Wilson, Stefanie Schroeder, Angela Guzman, and Hannah Cannon—for all your hard work and to Rebecca Matheson for organizing my vision for the book through words. Additional thanks to Micah Kandros, Richmond & Williams, and Milkglass Creative.

Thank you to all the people who made this project possible: Harold Weitzberg, Chad Christopher at SGSBC, the Gersh Agency, Rogers and Cowan, and Seven Artist Management. And last but not least, a special shout-out to Bailey Sexton and E. J. Hernandez.

INDEX

Photo Credits

PHOTOGRAPHY
Melissa Coulier

MAKEUP
Tara Brooks

HAIR
Daniel Blaylock

FASHION
Joseph Cassell & Erin MacDonald

PHOTOS BY MELISSA COULIER

vi, viii, 9, 39, 40, 46, 47, 49, 51, 59, 67, 68, 87, 113, 114, 124 *photos of Candace*, 126, 127, 128, 138 *photos of Candace*, 140, 141, 142, 143, 147, 148, 151, 154 *photos of Candace*, 157, 158, 160, 161, 162, 163, 164, 165, 176 *photo of Candace*, 188, 190, 191, 192, 193, 194, 195, 197, 198, 199, 200, 203, 206 *photo of Candace*, 211, 219

ADDITIONAL PHOTOS COURTESY OF CANDACE CAMERON BURE

x *purple overalls*, xv, 6 *top right/middle left*, 14 *all images except top left*, 17, 20 *black and white dress, red skirt, black and red dress*, 36 *top left/top right*, 42, 54 *top left/bottom right*, 79, 96, 166 *top left/middle right*, 167 *lower left/lower right*, 183, 235

ADDITIONAL PHOTOS BY MICAH KANDROS

6 *lower left*, 10, 13, 20 *lower right/upper right*, 29, 36 *middle right*, 43, 60, 63, 72 *top left/top right/middle right/bottom right*, 75, 76, 92 *middle right*, 104 *lower left/lower right*, 110, 116–117, 118, 124 *product photos*, 130, 134, 138 *product photos*, 145, 150, 154 *product photos*, 159, 169, 176 *top right/middle left*, 181, 185, 208, 216

ADDITIONAL PHOTO CREDITS

page x *overalls* © ZUMA Press, Inc./Alamy Stock Photo
        plaid shorts © Ron Galella, Ltd./WireImage/Getty Images

page 6 *hanging tops* © www.istock.com/I_rinka
        sunglasses © www.istock.com/CarmenMurillo
        Candace & Natasha © Jose Perez/startraksphoto.com

page 14 *black striped shirt* © Everett Collection Inc/Alamy Stock Photo

page 23 © Fernando Lucena/startraksphoto.com

page 24 *white skirt* © Roger Wong / INFphoto.com
         black/white skirt © Prandoni/BFA/REX/Shutterstock
         floral skirt © Barry King/Getty Images

page 26 © Jun Sato/WireImage/Getty Images

page 30 © WENN Ltd/Alamy Stock Photo

page 31 *lacy dress* © Frederick M. Brown/Getty Images
         white dress © Frederick M. Brown/Getty Images

page 32 *multi-colored dress* © Michael Loccisano/Getty Images for Alice + Olivia by Stacey Bendet
         black dress © Lucianna Faraone Coccia/FilmMagic/Getty Images

page 33 © Tibrina Hobson/FilmMagic/Getty Images

page 36 *long-sleeved dress* © Chelsea Lauren/REX/Shutterstock
         denim skirt © elenovsky/ Shutterstock

page 45 © Michael Tran/FilmMagic/Getty Images

page 54 *leather jacket* © depoo/Shutterstock
         jean jacket © Margarita Nikolskaya/Shutterstock

page 56 © www.istock.com/bonetta

page 62 © Stockforlife / Shutterstock

page 72 *navy sandals* © Nadiia Korol/Shutterstock
         canvas sneakers © www.istock.com/Denisfilm

page 82 clockwise from top left:
         white dress © WENN Ltd/Alamy Stock Photo
         makeup © Jason Merritt/Getty Images
         black dress © Jeffrey Mayer/WireImage/Getty Images
         orange dress © Jon Kopaloff/FilmMagic/Getty Images

page 84 © Broadimage/REX/Shutterstock

page 85 clockwise from top left:
         red dress © Astrid Stawiarz/Getty Images for AHA
         silver dress © Larry Busacca/Getty Images
         black/white dress © Jamie McCarthy/Getty Images for EJAF
         red/silver dress © Cindy Ord/Getty Images for Jaguar Land Rover

page 92 clockwise from top left:
         hangers © Life morning/Shutterstock
         stack of shirts © Africa Studio/Shutterstock
         closet © www.istock.com/KhongkitWiriyachan
         folded clothes © www.istock.com/Catherine Lane

page 95 *Dancing with the Stars* © Adam Taylor/ABC via Getty Images

page 104 *map* © www.istock.com/:Probuxtor
          passport © allstars/Shutterstock
          headphones © www.istock.com/Azure-Dragon

page 109 i viewfinder/Shutterstock

page 124 *towels* © www.istock.com/Floortje

page 166 clockwise from top left:
          braid © Vivien Killilea/Getty Images for DesignCare
          at salon © Gustavo Caballero/Getty Images
          red hair © Kevin Winter/Getty Images
          blue cardigan © ZUMA Press, Inc./Alamy Stock Photo

page 167 clockwise from top left:
          navy tanktop © Jason LaVeris/FilmMagic/Getty Images
          black/silver jumpsuit © ZUMA Press, Inc./Alamy Stock Photo
          black sweater © United Archives GmbH/Alamy Stock Photo

page 176 *veggie wrap* © Daxiao Productions/Shutterstock
          quinoa salad © Joshua Rainey Photography/ Shutterstock

page 183 *tea* © www.istock.com/amenic181

page 206 *coffee table* © www.istock.com/gregory_lee
          bath salts © Sea Wave/Shutterstock
          candle © Eli Maier /Shutterstock
          teacup © www.istock.com/TeerawatWinyarat

page 222 © X-tina/Shutterstock